I0469551

How to Start and Run an Online Business

By Christine John

How to Start and Run an Online Business

Email: christinejohnbooks@gmail.com

ISBN: 9781482637434

Disclaimer:

Although the author has made every effort to ensure that the information in this book was correct at press time, the author does not assume and hereby disclaims any liability to any party for any loss, damage, or disruption caused by errors or omissions, whether such errors or omissions result from negligence, accident, or any other cause.

Why You Need to Read This Book

The book you are reading right now will help you to start and run a successful internet business without emptying your wallet.

For three years I struggled and made so many mistakes when I first tried to build an internet business. I had dreams of resigning from my job, entering full self-employment, and making a profitable living online.

But because I was new to the whole cyber scene, and not having a more experienced person to help me avoid all the pitfalls, I really didn't have a clue what I was doing.

But I never gave up and neither should you. I made a lot of mistakes trying to set up an online business, but I also did a lot of research, read many articles and books on internet marketing and online business, and used all of the tips, tricks and advice that I picked up over the years to create this simple, yet powerful, step-by-step guide to help you to achieve your dream of starting an online business of your own.

Once people heard that I had started my own internet business, they asked me to help them to set up their business online, in which many of them have been very successful. For example, a taxi driver hired me to design and promote a website for him to persuade tourists to hire him to be their taxi driver and tour guide in which he would pick them up from the airport, take them to their hotel and provide guided tours around the island.

By using marketing methods such as video marketing, email marketing, site submission, and social media, my client's taxi and tour business increased and his revenue doubled in less than a month!

These internet marketing strategies worked for me and my customers, and they will work for you. All you need to do is follow the steps in this internet business guide and you will be on your way to generating revenue from your very own online business.

There are four ways this step-by-step guide can help you:

1. This book will show you exactly how you can start making money by creating a profitable online business. You will discover how to come up with profitable business ideas, how to do your market research and how you can find out what your prospective customers are interested in. This book will also show you what type of product to sell to your prospective customers, whether it is your own product or other people's products through affiliate marketing.

2. You will find step-by-step detailed instructions on how to create a website or blog. This book will show you how to register a domain name, set up web hosting, and how to design your website or blog. There is even a chapter that shows you how to set up an e-commerce website to sell your own products. This book will even show you how to avoid the mistakes I made when registering a domain name.

3. My internet business guide will show you how to promote your website online and offline. The marketing strategies that you will find in this book are the very same strategies I used to promote my business and I can assure you that these marketing methods will also work for you. Promoting your website is usually the most difficult part of building an online business and it can be very time-consuming and frustrating to attract customers to your site. But I am going to show you some very easy and cost-effective ways of promoting your business online that will help you to grow your business and increase your revenue.

4. If you have never started a business before, then you will love the chapters on how to write a business plan and register your business. Additionally, this book will show you how to keep accounting records and several different ways to turn your business into a profit-generating machine!

Depending on how much time you have, the strategies in this book could take you a few days or a few weeks to complete. I have set up an internet business action plan that will help you to stay focused on the tasks you have to perform in order to achieve your goal of starting your online business. I know you may be wondering how you are going to find time to follow the steps in this book, but I believe that it is well worth the time and effort it takes to achieve your goal of kissing your 9 to 5 job goodbye and becoming the boss of your own internet business.

You have already taken the first step towards becoming financially independent by reading this book. Now all you have to do is follow the strategies detailed in this book to help you to become a highly successful online entrepreneur. Now let us begin.

Table of Contents

Introduction

In this book you will discover how to succeed in starting a profitable online business. This book goes into full detail from coming up with a profitable idea and conducting your market research, to getting your business online and generating sales.

I assume that you bought this book because you are interested in starting an online business but just don't know how. I also assume you bought this book because you are either tired of your present job and want to be your own boss, you don't feel secure in your job and you believe that you will be made redundant, or you are unemployed and you are having great difficulty in finding another job. Maybe you are a stay-at-home parent and would like to start a business you can run from home. Or maybe you have heard so much about the success of other people who have started their online business that you decided to learn more about it and find out how you too can make a living online.

What is an Online Business?

I'm sure you have heard of Amazon, eBay, Yahoo and Facebook. These are a few examples of online businesses. To put it simply, an online business is any business that sells products, services and advertising on the internet.

There are many different types of online businesses. There are some physical businesses which sell their products online such as Tesco, Marks & Spencer, and Toys R Us. You will notice that these are all retail companies. There are auction sites which sell their products to the highest bidder such as eBay.com. Other online businesses use their websites to provide information, reports and reference material in digital format. Still there are other online businesses which offer web based services such as online banking and payment processing services.

Internet businesses are growing in popularity because the internet makes it so easy for anyone to start up an online business. You do not need to make a large investment and you could start your internet business in just a couple of days. The two main things you have to pay for are the domain name and web hosting.

Even if you are new to the internet and the thought of starting an online business seems too complicated to you, there are many books, videos, and software that you can use to guide you step by step through the start up phase of your online business. This book you are reading right now is one such example.

What are the Advantages and Disadvantages of Starting an Online Business?

Starting an online business has both advantages and disadvantages which you need to consider before making a commitment to this type of business venture.

Some advantages of starting an online business include:

1. You can be your own boss. You have full control over what you sell and how much you

charge for your products. Additionally, 100% of the profits belong to you.

2. If you are selling physical products, then you have no need to rent a building for a store and you do not need to hire sales staff.

3. You can operate your online business from your home. There is no need to commute.

4. You can sell all of your products directly from your website and ship them to your customers from one central location.

5. You can reach a larger target audience. You are not restricted to selling only to consumers located in your neighbourhood or local region.

6. You do not need a lot of money to start a business. Internet businesses are fast, cheap and easy to set up.

7. You do not need a large advertising budget. You can promote your online business for free very easily by producing a video, submitting articles to article directories, interacting with other web users on social networking sites, and creating slideshows.

Although there are many benefits to starting an online business, there are also some disadvantages which you should consider. Some disadvantages are as follows:

1. Promoting an online business can be very difficult, especially for new online business owners trying to establish their websites on the internet.

2. You will be competing with large businesses that have far greater resources than you do to drive customers to their sites.

3. Depending on what you're selling, your customers may prefer to purchase their goods from a physical store rather than ordering it online.
4. Because you are conducting business mainly on the internet you and your staff may have trouble developing relationships with your customers because you do not deal with them face to face. This could hurt your business in that your customers may be more inclined to make an in-person purchase rather than visiting your online store.

These are a few points that you should consider seriously before diving into an online business venture. Please do not let this information discourage you. I want you to keep an open mind and be aware of the benefits as well as the challenges you will face when setting up your online business.

Do You have What it Takes to Start and Run an Online Business?

Running an online business may seem like a very attractive idea, but it is not something that everyone can do. It takes certain skills and personal traits to make an online business successful. Read through the following personal traits and skills you need to run a business and then ask yourself, "Do you have what it takes to start and run an online business?"

You need to be passionate about what you do. Starting a business can be very challenging. If you don't love what you do then you are going to find it very difficult to persevere in your business venture when you face a few road blocks. It is hard to stay motivated if you are not passionate about your business. Therefore make sure that your business idea is one that you feel passionate about. Don't choose an idea simply because you think it will make you a lot of money. You should love what you plan to do or else your business will fail.

Secondly, when starting a business you will need to make a lot of sacrifices, especially in the first couple of years. It is going to take a lot of time and effort from coming up with a profitable idea to creating the product and establishing your business. You need to prepare yourself and your family for the hardships ahead. There are certain things you may have to give up while you are building your business such as family holidays, a new car, and TV time. You may have to work longer hours to get your business off the ground, much longer than you did when you were working at your 9-5 job. Furthermore, you may have to spend less time with your family and friends, less time on your hobbies and sports, and bring home a smaller salary than what you were making at your former job.

You will face risk and uncertainty. Whether you are planning to open a physical store or run a business on the internet, you will always face a certain level of risk. Running your own business means that you no longer have the security of a regular salary from an employer. It may be weeks, months, or even years before your business makes a profit or is able to pay you a decent salary. While you are working on getting your business off the ground, you need to make sure that your idea is profitable and that you have enough savings to live on, or at least remain in your current job, until your business starts making a profit.

Additionally, you need to have plenty of patience and persistence. Starting a business never goes exactly according to the plan. You will meet a few problems and stumbling blocks along the way. It is at this moment when you really need to have a lot of patience and the willingness to see the business through. Some challenges you may encounter are financial issues, problems with staff, computer malfunction, or difficult customers. No matter what hurdles you have to jump over, you need to have patience and persistence to make your online business successful.

There are some skills that you will need to have in order to start and run a successful online business. Some of these skills you may not have in the initial stages of your business. In this case, you have to make a decision on how you are going to acquire those skills. Are you going to receive training or are you going to hire people who have the necessary skills to contribute to the growth of your online business? These are things you need to think about carefully.

You will need the following skills to start and run your online business:

Market Research Skills – You need to be able to identify and understand your customers' needs and wants. You should have full understanding of the market you are entering and the actions of your competitors.

Money Management Skills – For this particular skill, a bit of training may be required in basic bookkeeping and accounting. You need to be able to determine when your business will break even, make financial projections, and calculate profit and loss of the business. You need to have a full understanding of your business's financial position.

Marketing and Sales Skills – No matter how brilliant you think your product or service is, no one is going to know about it unless you find a way to promote and sell your offerings to the public, whether online or offline. Therefore you need to have strong marketing and sales skills in order to effectively communicate to your potential customers about your offerings and to generate sales. You can either learn these skills yourself or hire someone to do it for you.

People Skills – If you decide to hire workers and if your business involves dealing with customers on the phone or in person on a daily basis, then it is important that you develop this skill so that you may be able to motivate your employees and deal with customers in a professional manner.

Negotiating Skills – You will need this skill if you are doing business with suppliers or trying to negotiate contracts with other companies. This skill will come in handy when you try to strike up the best deal or win a bid for a job.

If you feel that you don't have all of these skills, then I highly recommend that you do courses in all of these areas, even if you plan to hire someone to do the work for you. It is better for you to get training in these skills so that you may be able to monitor what your employees are doing and to run your business better.

Starting an online business can be both a challenging and rewarding experience. It is very challenging because of the level of risk involved, the uncertainty, and the lack of support, which can be very discouraging. But you can be sure that the rewards you gain are far greater than the sacrifices you made.

You have already taken the first step by reading this guide to help you get started. In the end, when you are finally able to leave that stressful 9-5 job and when you find yourself in a financially secure position, you will look back on this day and be grateful that you made the decision to get out of the rat race and to make your dream come true.

Chapter 1: Coming Up With a Profitable Idea

Where Can You Get Ideas From?

For would-be entrepreneurs, coming up with a brilliant business idea is the first step which is often the most difficult. But thinking of a business idea should be fun and the best part is that you don't have to worry about how much money it will cost to develop or how much time it will take to develop your idea. At this point, all you have to do is brainstorm.

But to help you along, there are some ways you can come up with good business ideas. You just need to know where to look.

You can come up with great ideas by examining your interests and hobbies, your work experience, any specialized knowledge you may possess, or by identifying problems other people may be facing and coming up with a solution to those problems.

What Ideas Can You Get From Interests and Hobbies?

What are you interested in? What do you enjoy doing in your spare time? Do you like kite-flying, stamp collecting, playing guitar or fishing? Do you enjoy knitting, sewing, or building houses out of popsicle sticks? Whatever you enjoy doing, you have the potential to turn your hobby or interest into a profitable business. Consider all the things you are good at and think of how you can make it into a business.

For example, let's say you love football. Think of all the business ideas you can come up with just by thinking about your favourite sport. You could sell football equipment, become an expert at football coaching, or sell football accessories such as t-shirts or jackets. You could also trade football cards of your favourite players or sell tickets to all the games. Can't you see how easy that was? The possibilities are endless!

Do You Have Any Work Experience?

If you have spent a number of years working in a particular industry, then I'm sure you must have developed certain skills on the job. For example, if you were working as a secretary and noticed that there were certain tasks that you felt could be done differently in a better way, then you may be able to use the skills you acquired to do a better job. You could start an online business offering your secretarial or administrative services. Maybe you have found a way to create spreadsheets or do data entry more efficiently.

You could be a babysitter, a typist, a florist, or a painter. There are bound to be customers that may be in need of your services. You could be making money online by offering these services on your website or blog.

What Specialized Knowledge do You Have?

You may have some type of special knowledge or skill that other people in your area may require. For example, you may be a psychologist, a dentist, a plumber, an electrician, a doctor, or a web designer. There may be hundreds, or even thousands, of potential customers searching for someone who specializes in any one of these skills. You could build an online business based on these specialized skills that you possess. You could write e-books, make video demonstrations, or conduct interviews. Just think of the different ways you can use your skills to create an online business.

Are There any Problems You Can Identify?

It is possible for you to come up with a good internet business idea by looking for solutions to everyday problems. Talk to your family, friends, church members, co-workers, or your next door neighbour. Join online forums, read newspapers and magazines, or check out Yahoo! Answers for problems web users may have and think of ways you could solve those problems. Many online businesses were created just by solving everyday problems.

Maybe there is an existing product that does not function properly. You could do research on that existing product and come up with a way to improve it, or you may just come up with a totally new product.

Do You Need Further Inspiration?

Still can't think of any good ideas to start an online business? Just look around you. There are many aspects of your life that can inspire you to come up with a good business idea. You can find inspiration just by doing the following:

1. Listening to the radio
2. Reading newspapers
3. Watching television
4. Taking a walk
5. Reading a comic book
6. Joining social networks like Facebook, Twitter, and LinkedIn
7. Watching videos on YouTube
8. Reading blogs
9. Talking to a stranger
10. Walking the dog
11. Playing with your kids
12. Going to school

If you still can't think of a good internet business idea there are still other things you can do to find inspiration. You can search online for industries that you may be interested in. You can also research potential target markets by doing the following:

i. Focus on what other people are buying online. You can do this by checking out Amazon and eBay. They both show related items that other people bought. For example, on Amazon just scroll down to the section that says "Customers Who Bought This Item also Bought...".

ii.   Keep yourself up to date with national and world news. Read the newspapers, watch the news on television, read news feeds online, listen to the news on the radio, etc.

iii.   Be a voracious reader. Read printed books, e-books, magazines, blogs, etc. on the topics you are interested in.

I recently visited Amazon, eBay, and Yahoo! Shopping and from these sites I compiled a list of currently popular items that customers purchase online. You could use this list as a stepping stone to coming up with a profitable idea that you can use to start your own internet business.

1. Tablets
2. Skiing Equipment
3. Playstation 3
4. Xbox 360
5. Women's Watches
6. NFL and NHL Fan Gear
7. Holiday Decorations
8. Internet Marketing
9. Health and Fitness
10. Cooking (Food and Nutrition)
11. PC and Video Games

The popular categories that people search at these sites tend to change every week. So check back at Amazon, eBay, and Yahoo! Shopping to find out what the latest popular categories are and what books made it on the bestsellers list.

When you have come up with a few business ideas, write them all down on a sheet of paper or in a notebook so you

don't forget. Examine all the ideas you have produced
and narrow them down to the simplest ones that you feel
capable of converting to an online business.
Once this is done, we will move on to the next step,
which is to identify your target market.

Chapter 2: How to Identify Your Target Market

Who are your potential customers? Who are you going to sell your products or services to? These are questions you should be asking yourself while you are preparing your product to sell to consumers. But before you can identify your target market you first need to understand what the term 'target market' means and how to select your niche.

What is a Target Market?

A 'target market' is defined as "a particular group of potential customers which a company focuses on to sell its products and services to through various marketing techniques". In order to ensure that you are aiming your business at the right audience, you need to be able to describe a typical consumer who will purchase your product.

You can start by asking the following questions:

1. Are your target customers male or female?
2. Are they adults or children?
3. What age group are you planning to target?
4. Where do they live?
5. Do they work or do they go to school?
6. If they work, what do they do for a living?
7. How much money do they make?
8. Are they part of a social club, a charity, or religious institution?

The more you know about your target market, the better you will be able to design your product or service to meet their specific needs or wants.

For example, let's say you have chosen to focus your online business on the health and fitness industry. To narrow it down, you have decided to create an exercise video for your potential customers. Now you need to find out to which consumer group you will aim your exercise video. Your task is to define your target market, i.e. describe the typical consumer you will be selling to.

You did your market research and you have come up with your target consumer. Your exercise video will be aimed at young mothers living in the UK, between the ages of 25 to 35, who want to get back into shape after having a baby.

You can take a step further by narrowing down your target market even more by choosing your niche.

What is a Niche Market?

You have probably heard that the best way to be successful online is by finding and focusing on a particular niche. A niche market is "a specific segment of the general market which one may choose to develop a solution to meet the needs of that particular segment". That segment, or niche, can become your potential customers.

The advantage of selecting your niche is that you may have discovered a particular area of the market which exists that other small businesses may not know about and which big companies would not bother exploring. This gives you the opportunity to develop a product or service that is needed in that niche and to dominate that corner of the market.

For example, you may be interested in providing yard maintenance services. You could corner the market and select a niche in which your business offers hedge cutting or tree cutting services.

Once you have chosen your target market or your niche, you now need to do more market research.

Chapter 3: How to Carry Out Your Market Research

After you have written down your best online business ideas, identified your target market and selected your niche, it is now time to do your research to find out if there is a market where you can turn your ideas into products and how profitable it will be if you launched your business in that particular market.

When you think of market research, you are probably thinking that it's going to be a lot of work. But market research is a very important tool that every business, whether new or existing, should use to find out what products and services will generate a profit. Researching the market is much easier now with Internet than it was back in the late 1980s to early 90s.

Over 30 years ago, before the Internet, you would have had to use the traditional marketing research methods to find your ideal customer. Some of these methods involved selecting a specific group (or sample) from the population, creating a questionnaire and interview questions, or forming focus groups, to find out from the public if they would be willing to buy whatever product or service your business was planning to offer. Additionally, you would have had to analyze data that has already been published to identify your competitors and your target market.

With the development of the Internet and the fact that it reaches a global audience, it has changed the way we do market research. Thanks to Google, Amazon, and eBay, and many other major online marketplaces, conducting market research has never been easier.

You may still have to create questionnaires and analyse existing data, but the high cost, time and effort it would have taken to do traditional research has been reduced significantly because of the Internet. You don't have to travel very far and you don't have to stop people on the street to ask them questions. You could visit the public library, but even this may not be necessary. All this can be done easily by doing your research online. But whether you like it or not, whether it's online or offline, you still have to do your research.

If you fail to do your market research before you start your online business, or even during its operation, then you will have no idea who your potential customers are, where you can find them, or when they will most likely and be willing to purchase your product or utilize your services. Failing to do research is like operating your business with your eyes closed. You need to know as much as you can about the market you are planning to do business in. Therefore, it is very important to conduct your market research.

How do You Research the Market?

In order to do your market research, there are three factors that you must keep in mind in order to verify that there is an existing market on the internet and that there is a significant demand for information that they search for it online. These three factors are:

1. What products, services, or information are in demand (Google Keyword Tool)
2. Determining profitability of your chosen market (Google Search Results)
3. Analysing the competition (Clickbank, Amazon, eBay)

Discovering what products or services are in demand on the web is essential to your market research. The best way to find out what's in demand is the **Google Adwords Keyword Tool**. It is very easy and free to use. You don't even need to sign up for an account to use this tool. Go to https://adwords.google.com/o/keywordtool.

For example, if you wanted to find out how many people searched for the keyword 'guitar lessons', just type in this phrase in the dialog box next to Word or phrase on the page where it says Find Keywords and click on the Search button.

Google Keyword Tool

Find keywords
Based on one or more of the following:

Word or phrase | One per line

Website | www.google.co.uk/page.html

Category | Apparel

☐ Only show ideas closely related to my search terms ?

⊞ Advanced Options and Filters

Locations: United Kingdom ✕   Languages: English ✕   Devices: Desktops and laptops

Type the characters that appear in the picture below.
Or sign in to get more keyword ideas tailored to your account.

USetsjr   usurping

Letters are not case-sensitive

Search

From the results for the keywords 'guitar lessons' you can see that there are 823,000 global monthly searches.

Search Results

Keyword	Competition		Global Monthly Searches ?	Local Monthly Searches ?
guitar lessons ▾	Medium		823,000	90,500

✓ Save all **Keyword ideas (100)**			1 - 50 of 100 ▾ ‹ ›	
Keyword		Competition	Global Monthly Searches ?	Local Monthly Searches ?
guitar lessons for beginners ▾		High	40,500	4,400
free online guitar lessons ▾		High	18,100	1,900
guitar lessons online ▾		High	49,500	6,600
free guitar lessons ▾		High	49,500	5,400
guitar lessons london ▾		High	5,400	4,400
guitar lesson ▾		Medium	673,000	74,000
online guitar lessons ▾		High	49,500	6,600

So you can see from the search results that there is a lot of interest in guitar lessons. Any search term that generates global monthly searches of 500 or more means that there may be money to be made in that particular niche.

The next part of your market research is determining the profitability of your chosen market. You can do this by using the Google search results. By this I mean typing keywords in the search box and then clicking the Search button.

A keyword is simply a word that someone uses to perform a search on the internet using a search engine such as Google, Yahoo, or Bing. Web surfers hope to use these keywords to describe what they are looking for on the web.

For example, if you go to www.google.com and type the keywords 'guitar lessons' in the Search box, you will find many results for this term. On the right side of the Google search results page, you will see about 8 sponsored ads. These are ads companies paid Google to display on the first page of search results. What this means is that your chosen niche, selling guitar lessons, is a very profitable niche because there are several companies in this niche that are paying a lot of money to attract customers to their site.

As I mentioned before, you could also visit the following websites to find out what products people are spending their money on:

http://www.yahooshopping.com
http://www.ebay.com
http://www.amazon.com

When you check out these websites pay close attention and make a list of the following:

1. The most popular products being purchased
2. The top lists showing which products or subjects are selling the most. You can also check the top book lists.
3. Take note of the other items that customers purchased. Amazon is a good example of this.
4. Check titles of various books to give you an idea of a niche market you may want to choose for your online business.

When you have completed your market research and have an idea of the market you want to start your internet business in, the next step is to decide what you are going to sell.

Chapter 4: Decide What You Are Going to Sell

This is the fun part of starting your online business. You need to decide on what products or services you are going to sell. You have two choices. You can either sell your own product or sell other people's products. There are advantages and disadvantages to selling your stuff and other people's stuff. After reading this section, you will need to decide what you are going to do.

Why Should You Create and Sell Your Own Product?

Normally, when you start a business offline (i.e. one that's not on the internet), you usually have a product or service of your own that you have created, or have the idea to create, and you want to market it to generate revenue for your enterprise.

One of the advantages of creating and selling your own product is that you will have full control. You can make all of the decisions on the form, design, packaging, and delivery of your product. Some other advantages include:

1. You get to be your own boss. You don't have anyone to be accountable to except yourself.
2. Most of the money you make from marketing and selling your own product belongs to you. In other words, you keep most of the profits from every sale.
3. You know your product inside out, therefore you are able to promote your product with confidence,

knowing its contents well and thus gaining the trust of your customers.

4. You can make others work for you, selling your product.
5. You learn something new when doing research for your product.
6. You become an expert at what you do. For example, if you are interested in building model airplanes, and you do plenty of research on the topic, in time you may become an expert and be able to help other people too.

Although there are benefits to creating and selling your own product, there are also drawbacks. The following are difficulties you may face when trying to create and sell your own product:

1. You won't make any money for your business if your product is not ready to sell.
2. All of the costs incurred to create your product, to promote it and to sell it belong to you.
3. It takes time to create and develop your own product. It could take months or even years.

In spite of the disadvantages, which are very few, I would still recommend creating your own product or service to market and sell. The reason is that it gives you the best chance of success in running your online business.

What Type of Product Should You Create?

There are many different types of products that you can create. You can create physical goods or digital products. But the easiest one to create is an information product, or info product for short. You can produce an info product very easily with not as much effort as you would if you were building a physical product, and you can make money from it in the shortest amount of time.

There are many different types of info products that you can produce. Because of the rate at which technology is developing every year, you are given a variety of ways to come up with info products which you can deliver to your potential online customers. You can explore the following examples of info products that you can create in a short amount of time:

Special Report – It should be filled with high quality information which you can give away for free or charge a low fee. It can be in the form of an audio, video, or written report which can be downloaded instantly.

Getting-Started Kit – You can package this product by putting together a series of special reports and include a CD or DVD to sell to your customers.

Home-Study Course – This usually consists of a manual, a few audio CDs and some special reports. This is a great money-generator for your online business.

Sample Newsletter – You can write a single page of great content or 10 to 15 pages which touch on various topics. You can email a sample of your newsletter to your readers so that they may get an idea of what your site is all about and what products you are selling. They will also have an idea of what they are missing.

Book – You can either publish a book in printed form or as a PDF version. This is a great info product to create if you want to become a published author. It also shows your readers your knowledge and expertise on a particular topic.

Interview Series Transcript – Interview different experts on a particular topic and then sell the interviews on your website. You can also allow your customers to download MP3 audios or transcripts of the interviews.

Quick-Start Guide – Your customers may feel overwhelmed by the vast information offered in a home study course that they don't know how to begin or where to start. You could include a quick-start guide which summarizes what the whole course is about and the first steps to get started.

CD – You can provide your special report on CD for your customers to listen to. It can be an audio CD or a short video.

Free Video – You can use Windows Movie Maker, your digital camera, or some other software to produce your own video. You can submit it to YouTube.com or other websites which can be viewed online for free. Your video can be about a product you are promoting, your website, or about your online business.

Teleseminar/Webinar – In a teleseminar a group of people listen to an interview or presentation on the telephone. A webinar is similar to a teleseminar except that people follow the interview or presentation on their computers. You can also make a transcript of the teleseminar or webinar and sell it with the audio of the call.

These are just a few examples of info products that you can create easily and inexpensively. There are many other info products which are not listed here but you could easily learn more about them by checking other websites in your niche or by doing a keyword research on one of the major search engines such as Google.

Should You Sell Other People's Products?

Selling other people's products on the internet is called Affiliate Marketing, and yes, it is possible to make money this way. If you cannot come up with your own idea for a product that you want to create and sell, then this is the next best option you have. You can sell existing products and services until you have created your own product. In fact, you can do both – sell your own product as well as affiliate products.

What is Affiliate Marketing?

Affiliate marketing is a process whereby you earn a commission by selling existing products and services for other companies online. You can place a text ad, banner, or link on your website. When a visitor to your site clicks on a banner, for example, they will be taken to the sales page of one of the affiliate products that you are promoting. If the person buys a product from that site then you will earn a percentage of that sale as commission.

You can find affiliate programs in almost any niche you choose to develop your business in. You can earn money from selling your own products as well as affiliate products. When promoting affiliate products, the more sales you make, the more commission you are paid.

There are several advantages and disadvantages to promoting affiliate products. Some advantages include:

1. Affiliate marketing is an easy way to earn additional income.
2. Affiliate marketing can be done anywhere in the world as long as you have a computer and internet connection.
3. Starting affiliate marketing can be done with very little or no technical knowledge whatsoever.
4. You can keep your regular job while you establish yourself as an affiliate marketer. It will not interfere with your job.
5. The product and its marketing material have already been created by the merchant (the seller), which saves you a lot of time and money.
6. You don't have to worry about processing or shipping orders, or processing payments because the merchant handles all these aspects of the sale.
7. You receive a lot of advice and tips from the merchants on how to promote their products.

Although affiliate marketing can be a very lucrative business, there are some disadvantages which you should take into consideration before taking on this venture. The following are disadvantages of affiliate marketing:

1. You do not have any control over the products you sell because they do not belong to you.
2. It may take a few months before you ever receive a commission.
3. You cannot start your own affiliate program for products you don't own.
4. You might recommend a poor quality product which could result in losing the trust of your existing customers.
5. A merchant might shut down an affiliate program without informing the affiliates and may not pay your commission.

Don't allow all these limitations of affiliate marketing stop you from becoming an affiliate marketer. It is possible to make money from affiliate marketing. You just need to do your research and make sure you examine the contracts and understand how affiliate marketing works before you jump into it.

How Do You Get Started in Affiliate Marketing?

If you own a website or a blog, one of the great ways to generate revenue is through affiliate marketing. Although many online marketers talk about how lucrative affiliate marketing can be, it is not that easy to earn an income when you first get started. But don't let this worry you too much. The key to cashing in with affiliate marketing lies in the following factors:

1. You may need to have your own website or blog.
2. Your site must have a lot of traffic, i.e. a lot of web surfers are visiting your site frequently.
3. Your readers should be in a buying mood.
4. You need to find products which are relevant to your site. For example, if you're site is about dogs, then you could advertise affiliate products such as dog food, leashes, flea and tick shampoo, etc.
5. Ensure that the products you promote on your site are high quality products. This can be done by reading reviews of the products.
6. You need to be able to write good sales copy in order to promote affiliate products.
7. You need to build trust with your readers.

Once your website or blog is established and you are generating traffic to your site, you can begin by researching affiliate programs. Here are a few affiliate programs you can check out just to get you started:

Clickbank http://www.clickbank.com
Affiliate Window http://www.affiliatewindow.com
Commission Junction http://www.cj.com
Link Share http://www.linkshare.co.uk

You can choose to place banner ads on your site, text links, or you can select the exact products you would like to feature on your site.

There are some big name companies that also offer affiliate programs which you can set up within minutes regardless of how well established your site is. Two of these popular companies are eBay and Amazon. With Amazon, you can choose from a wide variety of ads or choose Amazon products that you want to feature on your site. With eBay, you can select specific products from eBay's auctions to advertise on your site.

If you live the UK, to join Amazon's Associates Program, go to http://www.amazon.co.uk. Go to Amazon.com if you live in the US. Scroll down to the bottom of the page and click Associate's Program under "Make Money with Us". Follow the instructions to join the Associates Program. You can read more detailed instructions on how to join Amazon by reading Chapter 6.

If you want to join eBay's affiliate program, then go to http://www.ebay.co.uk (UK residents) or eBay.com (US residents). Scroll down to the bottom of the page and click Affiliates under "About eBay". Then click on the Apply Now grey button located on the top right side of the screen under "Apply Now to the eBay Partner Network". And then follow the steps to becoming part of eBay's Partner Network.

When you join any one of these affiliate programs, always make sure that you read the contract, terms and conditions, and make sure you understand how you will be paid, how much, and how often. And that's all there is to getting started with affiliate marketing.

Chapter 5: Create a Website

A website is a collection of web pages which contain text files written in a computer language called HTML that describes how a page should be formatted when it is displayed on your computer screen. A typical website may consist of several pages such as Home, About Us, Contact, Products page, and a Blog.

You also have the option of creating a simple blog. A blog is short for weblog. At first a blog was like an online diary which a person used to talk about personal things going on in their lives. Now it has become so much more than that. A blog is simply a collection of commentary posted on the internet. If you do an online search you will find blogs written on a wide variety of topics such as personal, political, photographic, corporate, news, and so much more. Blog posts are usually displayed in reverse chronological order with the newest posts displayed at the top. Readers are able to write comments which are posted at the bottom of the blog post for everyone to see.

There are a few essential items that you will need in order to create a website such as a domain name, a web host, and an autoresponder. I will explain each of these terms as we go through each of the steps to creating your own website.

Step 1: Register Your Domain Name

When you open your web browser (e.g. Internet Explorer), you see http://www.google.com on your address bar. Google.com is the domain name. It is a unique address used on the internet to find a particular web page or website.

Before you can create a website you need to first come up with a proper domain name for your site and then register it at a domain name registering company. Here are a few tips for coming up with a great domain name.

1. Try to come up with words related to your niche market or the type of online business you want to create. Write down as many words as you can.
2. You can use a dictionary and a thesaurus to find as many words as you can to come up with your domain name.
3. Use the Keyword Tool provided by Google to search for domain names. Type a name in the search box and see how many people have searched for information pertaining to that particular keyword. Based on the results you can use that keyword as your domain name.

Once you are satisfied with your domain name, you can then register it at your chosen domain name registrar company. There are many domain registration companies online, but the one I use is Domainorb.com. You pay less than $10 per year for your domain name. If you are looking for something cheaper, or want a co.uk domain, then you can go to Names.co.uk to register it. GoDaddy.com is another domain registration company that you can use as well.

How to Register a Domain Name

To register your domain name go to
http://www.domainorb.com. Enter your domain name in
the form and click Check it! If the domain name you have
chosen is unavailable, then click Search Again. Enter
another domain name, ensure that .com is selected, and
click Submit. When you find a domain name that is
available, click Update Selections/Continue. Click
Checkout and then fill in the forms in which you enter
your Login and Contact information, and Domain
Registration Contact Info.

You can leave the last section about Nameservers blank.
You will enter this information later after you purchase
web hosting. When you have completed the form you can
then click Submit. You will then be taken to the
2Checkout web page, also known as 2CO, where you will
enter your credit card details to purchase your domain
name. An email will be sent to confirm that your domain
name registration was a success.

There are two important points that you must keep in mind when you register a domain name:

You may not transfer a domain name for 60 days after its purchase or for 60 days after you change any registrant contact information. This rule was set by the Internet Corporation for Assigned Names and Numbers (ICANN) and this is a standard rule for all domain name registrars. For example, if you registered a domain name at Domainorb.com and wanted to transfer the domain name to a web host such as Dreamhost.com, then you would have to wait 60 days before you can transfer your domain name. Also if you changed your address after you registered your domain name then you cannot transfer the domain name for 60 days.

You should not register your domain name with the same company you are going to purchase web hosting from. The reason is that you may face problems in the future when you decide that you no longer want to use that company's web hosting services and want to transfer your domain name to a different web host. For example, if you registered your domain name at Webhost1.com and also purchased web hosting services from that site, and you wanted to transfer your domain name to Webhost2.com, then webhost1.com might give you problems and may not want to let you transfer your domain name so easily. You might be charged a lot of money to transfer your domain name or go through a lot of trouble to unlock it so that you can transfer it. Therefore, always keep your domain name with your domain registrar. That way you always have control of your domain name and you can assign it to another web host if you are dissatisfied with the one you're with.

Step 2: Select a Web Host

A web host is a type of internet hosting service which stores your website and then transmits it on the internet for people to view. There are thousands of companies on the internet offering web hosting services. For a new online entrepreneur trying to start an internet business, finding a good web host can be a little overwhelming. It may be tempting to purchase cheap hosting services from a web host, but you should not select a web host based on price alone. There are other factors you should consider before choosing a company to host your website or blog.

1. The web host you choose should be reliable and provide support immediately. If you have a problem with your website, you want a web host that will respond quickly to your query. Look for a web host that provides 24/7 support.

2. Ensure that your web host has PHP version 5.2.4 or greater and MySQL version 5.0 or greater. PHP is a scripting language that is suitable for web development. MySQL is a database management system which you can use to add, access and process data stored in a computer database. A database is a structured collection of data such as a shopping list, a picture gallery or information from a corporate network.

I recommend the following web hosts to host your domain:

http://www.JustHost.com
http://www.BlueHost.com
http://www.Hostgator.com

How to Set Up Web Hosting

I use Justhost.com to host my domain so I will show you how to set up your domain on the same web host. First, go to http://www.justhost.com and click Sign Up. Select "I already own my domain (transfer clients)". Enter your domain name, e.g. yournameforever.com and click Continue. Then enter your Contact information and Payment information. Ensure that the check box next to Confirmation is selected. This ensures that you have read and agree to the terms and conditions of use.

Then choose your account plan. The Hosting Essentials, such as the Site Backup Pro, SiteLock, and Search Engine Jumpstart, are optional. You can select the ones you feel you need, but I would not recommend purchasing any of them at this time. Then click Complete. An email will be sent to you to confirm that your web hosting has been set up. The web host will also include the Nameservers to use to link your domain name to your web host.

Step 3: Set Your Domain Name DNS

DNS stands for Domain Name Server. It is also referred to as simply Nameserver for short. Once you have set up hosting services your web host would have emailed you the DNS information.

Once you have the information just go to the site where you registered your domain name and update the nameserver records. Your domain registrar will provide instructions on how to do this. Enter the DNS information that your web host gave you. It looks like this:

NS1.hostname.com
NS2.hostname.com

It may take up to 48 hours for the nameservers to take effect and to propagate the internet, but when it is done your domain name will be linked to your web host. Also when you type your domain name in the address bar of your web browser you will be able to see your website live on the web.

For example, let's say you recently registered the domain name Myguitarlessons4u.com at Domainorb.com. You now want to link your domain name to your web host, which is webhosttoday.com. First, you need to go to http://www.domainorb.com and click Member Login. Enter your username and password and click Submit.

Next, click View/Edit next to "Number of domains in your account". Then click the letter 'M', which stands for 'Manage', in the third column in the same row as your domain name. Click 'Change Nameservers'.

Next to the word 'Use' select 'Custom Nameservers' from the drop down menu. In the first text box enter: ns1.webhosttoday.com. In the second text box enter: ns2.webhosttoday.com. Then click Submit. The page will then say 'Dns modification success'. Then click Logout and you're done. You just have to wait about 48 to 72 hours for your domain name to be linked to your web host and become active on the internet.

Step 4: Design Your Website

You could use the site builders offered by your web host, but I recommend using Wordpress to design your site because it is simple and you can build a site in a matter of minutes. With Wordpress you can create either a website or a blog or both.

Wordpress started off as a free web-based software program that could be used to set up and maintain a website or blog. But now Wordpress has grown into a content management system (CMS) which anyone can use to create a full-sized, social-media rich business website.

To set up Wordpress you need to go through your web host. Just click on the Wordpress icon on the cPanel. A page will open giving you instructions on how to install the software. Simply follow the instructions and your Wordpress site will be set up in a few minutes. An email will be sent to you with the login details to enter your Wordpress site.

To login to Wordpress, simply type in your address bar:

http://www.yoursite.com/wp-admin (Replace 'yoursite' with your domain name)

Enter your login details such as your username and password in the Wordpress dialog box as shown below:

Here is a brief overview of the menu functions and features of Wordpress. This information will assist you in designing your Wordpress site.

Dashboard – It is the control panel where you can manage your comments, publish your content, and many other things. The dashboard operates behind the scenes of your site. It is referred to as the "back end" of your site that only you can see.

The "front end" is what the outside world can see when they visit your site. You will be using the tools on your dashboard to change the appearance of your site and to publish content.

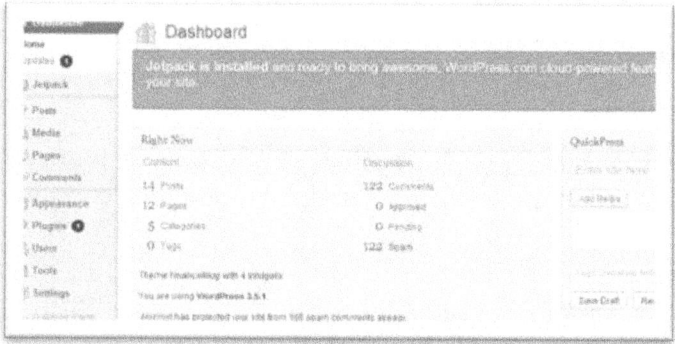

General Settings – Click Settings and General to change the title and tagline for your site. You can also adjust other general settings such as your email address, language, etc.

Appearance – When someone visits the home page of your Wordpress site, they are looking at the "front end" of your site, that is, the appearance of your site. You can change the way your site looks by downloading and installing a different Wordpress theme. Click on Appearance under the dashboard menu and then click Themes. You can change the theme by clicking on one of the pre-installed themes and then clicking Activate.

However, if you want to use a different theme then you can do a Wordpress theme search in Google. There are many websites which offer free Wordpress themes. These are some of the websites I visit to find professional-looking Wordpress themes which you can download for free:

http://www.freewordpressthemes4u.com
http://www.themesbase.com

http://www.themesjunction.com

Select the theme you want and click Download. The theme will download to your computer hard drive as a Zip file. Under Themes in your Wordpress site, click the Install Themes tab and then click Upload. Click Choose File and select the file where you saved it on your hard drive. And then click Install Now. It takes only a few seconds for the file to upload to your site. Click Activate to change the theme and make it live on your site.

Widgets – These are different, but very useful, tools that you can use to put content on your site without having to learn any complicated codes. Widgets normally appear on the Sidebar of your Wordpress site. Once again click Appearance under the dashboard menu and then click Widgets. A page will open showing various widget buttons. Each widget has its own function and you can select the one you want to use according to your site's needs. Just drag a widget from the widget area to the target sidebar and drop it where you want it to appear.

For example, you can drag and drop a text widget into the sidebar area and then type something in the text area. Click Save and then close. The widget will appear on the sidebar of your site.

Pages – These are similar to posts in that they have a title and body text, but they are different in that they are not a part of the chronological blog stream. Click Pages under the Dashboard menu and Add New to create a new page on your site. This is where you would create a new page for Contact, About Us or Products page. These pages are known as static pages, in that they are not placed in chronological order like the blog posts.

Posts – Just like pages, posts have a title and body text where you can type your content. These posts appear in chronological order starting with the newest post at the top and the oldest post at the bottom. These posts make up what you call a blog and you can show up to 20 posts on your blog if you want to. Just click on Posts under the dashboard menu and click Add New to create a new post. Type in your information and click Publish. Your post will be published immediately on your site for the entire world to see.

Plugins – These are Wordpress tools that you can use to enhance certain functions of your site. There are plugins you can use to create forms, to block spam comments, to optimize your site, and so much more. To install a plugin, click on Plugins under the dashboard menu and click Add New. Type in a keyword and click Search Plugins. When you find the one you want, click Install Now and the plugin will be immediately installed onto your site. Click Activate to make the plugin active and then you can edit the plugin the way you want it. Instructions on how to use the plugin are usually included when it is installed in Wordpress, or you can go to the official website of the plugin you installed. The newly installed plugin will appear somewhere under the dashboard menu when it has been activated.

Here are a few examples of plugins that I have used on my site:

Akismet – one of the most popular spam blocker plugins for Wordpress. You need to sign up for a free Wordpress.com account to get an API key so that you can install and activate this plugin.

All in One SEO Pack – use this plugin to optimize your site for the search engines.

Exclude Pages from Navigation – this plugin allows you to hide or exclude pages from the primary navigation. In other words, the excluded pages will not appear as part of the menu bar on your site.

Fast Secure Contact Form – this plugin allows you to insert a contact form on your Contact page. The form consists of Name, Email, and text area for the user to write a message. It also has a Submit button.

Add an Image – You can upload an image to be inserted into your blog post or page. Make a new page or post, and in the editing section of your page click Upload/Insert. On the Add Media page, click Select Files. Go to your folder where you have saved your photos or pictures and select the one you want to insert. You can then type in a title and alternate text for the picture. Next to Alignment select where you want the picture to be displayed on the page, whether left, right, or in the centre. Next choose the size of the picture and then click Insert Into Post. Click Publish, if you are publishing the page for the first time, or click Update if you are making changes to the page.

Reading Settings – Under the dashboard menu, click Settings and then click Reading. This is where you can change the display of your front page. You can either have your blog appear on the front page or on a static page. If you want a static page to be on the front page then you first need to create a page for your blog. You can use Blog as the title of your page. You can also create a static page and call it Home. Then, next to Front Page Displays select a Static Page and select Home for the Front Page and Blog for the Posts Page. Scroll down to the bottom of the page and click Save Settings.

Comments – Visitors to your site have the option of leaving a comment after reading your blog. You may receive positive comments, negative comments, or spam. The Comments menu under the dashboard allows you to manage comments that come into your site. You can easily delete the comments you don't want to appear below your blog and select those which you consider to be spam.

You can also go to http://learn.wordpress.com to learn about the various functions used to set up your website with Wordpress,

On your website, you can include the following pages:

Home Page – This is the main page that people will see when they first visit your site. Use this page to describe what your site is about. You can include photos on the home page and a brief description of the other pages on your site. You can also provide a link that people can click on to visit the other pages on your site.

About Us – Visitors to your site may want to know more about you and your company. This is where you can provide more details about your online business. You can include information about the founders of the business, the types of products and services you offer, and explain what makes your business different from others. You can also include your company's mission statement, if you have one.

Product or Service Description – This may be too long a name for your web page so you can use the name "Products", "Store" or "Marketplace" to let your visitors know that you have items to sell. If you have only a few products you may need only one page. However, if you have hundreds or even thousands of products listed then you will need a lot more pages. Your products should be listed under Categories and each category should have its own page. In fact, to make things easier, you could set up an ecommerce section on your site. You can read more about this later.

Contact – If your customers want to get in contact with you, then you will need to provide a page with your physical address, phone number and email address. You can also place a contact form on the page where people can enter their information and it will be sent to your email address.

Blog – This is optional if you want to include a blog page on your site. You can do this easily with Wordpress. Your blog may contain content that is relevant to your site. You can write product reviews or book reviews, promote affiliate products, write about the latest news stories, or any other information that you feel your web visitors would be interested in reading.

Other pages that you should have on your site, but which may not be displayed in the navigational menu bar at the top of your site are:

Privacy Policy – This is a legal document or statement which declares a company's policy on how it collects, uses, manages and releases personal information about a customer or client. Personal information is anything that can be used to identify an individual such as the person's name, address, date of birth, marital status, telephone number, credit card information, etc. The privacy policy informs the visitor what information is collected, and whether it is kept confidential, shared with partners, or sold to other companies.

Go to the following websites to download a free privacy policy template:

http://www.surgedigital.co.uk/tools/website-privacy-policy-template
http://www.hostnorth.co.uk/privacypolicy.asp

Terms and Conditions – A contract or legal agreement which states general rules, special arrangements, provisions, requirements, specifications and standards of a business or website which a typical user must adhere to.

Go to the following websites to download a free copy of the terms and conditions template:

http://www.hostnorth.co.uk/privacypolicy.asp
http://www.entrepreneur.com/formnet/form/1174

Copyright Notice – This is a symbol (©) or a phrase which informs the user of an individual's or organization's claim to copyright ownership of published work, such as a website, an e-book or printed book, music, painting, photo, etc.

Go the following website to download a free copy of a copyright template:

http://explainafide.com.au/book-copyright-template

Disclaimer – This is a statement made by an individual or organization which disclaims, denies, disowns, or renounces a title, claim, interest, estate, or trust.

Go to the following website to download a free copy of a disclaimer template:

http://www.thebookdesigner.com/2010/01/6-copyright-page-disclaimers-and-giving-credit

Some examples of websites designed using Wordpress are:

http://www.myusedbooksforyou.com
http://www.overcomedomesticviolence.com
http://www.blackwomenpoetry.com

Step 6: Set Up Email Autoresponder for Your Site (Optional)

You want to keep customers coming back to your site and remind them of what you have to offer. This is what is known as follow-up emails. This can be done with an email autoresponder. An autoresponder is computer software which you can use to send emails to people automatically. What you do is set up a sequence of prewritten emails that are sent out to potential customers on your database at regular intervals. If people subscribe to your website you can send follow-up emails to them using your autoresponder to promote new products or to provide a link to your blog or newsletter.

It is not mandatory that you set up an autoresponder on your website. There are many websites that don't have autoresponders but are still very successful in promoting their products and services to their target audience. But if you do decide to add an autoresponder to your site, then you can either pay a monthly fee for an autoresponder or you can install a free Wordpressautoresponder plugin. A plugin is a tool which can increase the functionality of your Wordpress site.

You can search for autoresponder plugins at http://www.wordpress.org/extend/plugins. The following are some autoresponder plugins that I found at Wordpress.org that you can install on your site:

CF7 AutoresponderAddon
BFT Autoresponder
S2Member to WP Autoresponder Integration Plugin

You can also visit the following websites and sign up for their service:

Feedburnerhttp://www.feedburner.com
Aweberhttp://www.aweber.com
Constant Contact http://www.constantcontact.com
Get Response http://www.getresponse.co.uk
Mail Chimp http://mailchimp.com

There you have it. Just follow these simple steps and you will have your very own website set up and fully functional in just a few days.

Chapter 6: Create an E-Commerce Website

I included this section because you may have physical products that you want to sell on your website and a blog is simply not enough to sell products for your online business. You may also want to promote affiliate products on your site and just creating a link to the affiliate site is not enough. Instead of a blog, you can create an e-commerce store for your website. It can be either a web page or it can be a fully integrated e-commerce website.

E-commerce is short for electronic commerce. To put it simply, e-commerce is the buying and selling of goods and services by consumers and businesses on the internet.

There are two ways you can build an e-commerce website. If you are using Wordpress you can install a plugin for your site to sell your own physical or digital products or you can sign up for a free Amazon store which can be embedded into your website easily.

Install a Wordpress Plugin to Create an E-commerce Store

An excellent plugin that you can use to set up your online store is the WP Online Store plugin. This ecommerce plugin comes fully loaded with hundreds of great features and you can install it into any Wordpress theme. Setting up your very own fully operational online store is very easy with this impressive plugin.

The WP Online Store plugin has a lot of features which make running your ecommerce site very easy and beneficial to your business. Some of the features included in this plugin are as follows:

1. You can list an unlimited number of products and categories.
2. You can sell physical (shippable) and virtual (downloadable) products.
3. You can offer discount coupons to your customers.
4. It has a quick start menu so that you can get the essential tasks done quickly.
5. It comes with its own customer registration and login system with email verification, profile and order history.
6. It has a simple control panel, which allows you to easily add, edit, and delete products, images, categories and more.
7. It has a built in HTML newsletter system with mass email software which allows you to email your entire customer list from within your admin area.

There are many other features which just cannot be listed here, but you get the idea of how great this plugin is for anyone who wants to create an ecommerce store for their online business.

To install the WP Online Store plugin, just go to the plugins page in the admin area of your Wordpress site and click install. The instructions for finding and installing plugins were explained earlier in chapter 5.

There are other Wordpress ecommerce plugins that you could try such as:

WooCommerce
MarketPress
The CartPress e-Commerce Shopping Cart
Ready! e-Commerce Shopping Cart

If you don't have any physical or digital products of your own to sell as yet, but you still want to create an online store, then your other option is to join the Amazon Associates Program and use the tools provided by the company to build your e-commerce store selling products for Amazon.

The Amazon Associates program is an affiliate marketing program that allows you, as a website owner or blogger, to earn a commission by creating and placing links on your site so that customers can click on the link and buy products from Amazon. You earn a commission each time a customer clicks through and purchases an item from Amazon.

When you join the associates program, you not only get access to the tools needed to create an online store featuring any of Amazon's products, you can also use links, banners, and widgets on your site to promote Amazon. You can join the program for free and you can set up an online store in minutes.

How do You get Started with the Amazon Associates Program?

You can create an ecommerce store by first joining the Associates Program. The following steps show you what to do:

Step 1: Go to www.amazon.co.uk.

Step 2: Scroll down to the bottom of the page and click "Associates Program".

Step 3: Click "Join now for FREE!"

Step 4: Type in your email address and select "I am a new customer" and then click "Sign in using our secure server".

Step 5: Type in your name, email address and password. Then click "Create Account".

Step 6: Type in Payee Name, Address, and Phone Number. Select who will be the main contact for the account and select whether you are VAT registered or not. If you are VAT registered, then enter the VAT registration number. Then click "Next: Your Website Profile".

Step 7: Enter all the information about your website. Make sure you read the Associates Operating Agreement and then click Finish.

Step 8: You will be given your Associates ID. Scroll down the page and click "Specify Payment Method Now".

Step 9: Select your payment method. UK residents cannot be paid by cheque, so select "Pay Me by Direct Deposit".

Step 10: Enter your bank details and click Continue. You will then be taken to the Associates control page where you can use the tools provided by Amazon to monetize your site, i.e. make your site an income generating machine.

Step 11: Finally, click the "Get Started Now" button to learn more about the Amazon Associates Program and how you can set up your ecommerce store.

To build your own ecommerce store on your website selling products from Amazon, first click on the aStore tab above and then click 'Add an aStore'. Follow the instructions and once your aStore is complete you can copy and paste the link on to your website.

Once you have set up your online store and you are satisfied that it is fully operational, you can now move on to the next step which is to process credit card payments on your website.

Accept Credit Card Payments

The most essential part of setting up an e-commerce store is that you have to be able to accept credit card payments online. Thanks to many payment processing sites, you don't have to make any large investments in payment processing software or setting up a merchant account through your bank.

PayPal.com

If you want to send money, receive money, make online payments or set up a merchant account, then PayPal is the way to go. It is one of the fastest, easiest and safest ways to perform financial transactions on the internet.

PayPal is a global ecommerce payment processing gateway that allows you to make payments and money transfers through the internet. It performs online payment processing for online vendors (sellers), auction sites such as eBay, and other commercial sites for which it charges a fee.

You can sign up with PayPal for free and easily set up a business account in which you are given the ability to accept credit card payments online. You do not need to have any programming skills and there are no set-up or monthly fees. You can start selling online in minutes by simply adding payment buttons to your site. PayPal's Website Payments Standard allows your customers to move through the checkout securely and quickly. You can get started right away by first opening a business account at http://www.paypal.com.

Google Checkout

Google Checkout is an online payment processing service that simplifies the way people shop online. Google Checkout is a fast and secure way to allow your customers to buy from your online store by simply entering their username and password. The benefit of using Google Checkout is that once your customers have set up a Google account, all of their credit card details are stored on their account which means that they do not have to keep setting up a new account every time they buy from your online store. They just need to enter their username and password.

Google Checkout provides you with various tools that you can use to integrate it on your website. You can use Google Checkout to add Buy Now buttons to your site if you only sell single items, integrate it with other ecommerce providers, or send invoices and collect payments.

Start making online payments by signing up with Google Checkout at https://checkout.google.com/sell.

2Checkout

2Checkout is another online payment processing service that combines a payment gateway and a merchant account into a single package, which can be easily integrated with your site. 2Checkout provides global credit card processing in dozens of currencies and languages so you can sell your products all over the world.

2Checkout can be easily integrated with many of the popular online shopping carts such as OSCommerce, BigCommerce, ZenCart, CubeCart and Magento. Just pick your shopping cart and have your payment processing service set up in a matter of minutes. Also with 2Checkout you can sell digital products, physical products, and set up recurring billing services for your customers who pay subscription fees to gain access to your website.

To learn more about 2Checkout and to sign up, go to http://www.2checkout.com.

Chapter 7: Promote Your Website

In this section, we will look at the various methods of promoting your site so that you will be able to attract the right visitors to your website. This is the part where most entrepreneurs and individuals who are new to online business seem to have the most difficulty – that is, getting people to visit their site.

Promoting your site does not have to be some complicated marketing strategy. You just need to understand the various marketing methods used online and work on each one, one at a time. You don't need to have a large marketing budget and, for most of the methods, you don't even need to spend any money at all. We will examine each of the marketing methods and where to go and how to get started promoting your online business to attract targeted potential customers to your site.

Search Engine Optimisation

Search engine optimization (SEO) is all about getting your website or blog to appear in the top ten search results of the major search engines like Google, Bing and Yahoo! If you have used search engines regularly then you should understand how important it is for your site to appear on the first page of search results. It may seem like search engine optimization is a complicated task, but it is possible to optimize your site for the search engines by following these simple steps.

Step 1: Optimize your site with keywords that are relevant to your site. Remember, a keyword is a word used to perform a search on a search engine. Think of all the keywords relevant to your site.

For example, let's say you're interested in football and you have decided to create and sell an info product teaching beginners the rules of the game. You would come up with words and phrases such as "football", "football techniques", "learn to play football", "football tips", "football training", and "football rules". These keywords are terms which are relevant to the information on your site.

You don't need to use all of these keywords on one page of your site. If you have a blog or a large website, then you can use these keywords by posting articles on your site. If you want your targeted customers to find your site using the search term "football tips", for example, you can write an article optimized for that phrase. Place this key phrase in the title of your article: "Five Football Tips to Improve Your Game".

Step 2: Place keywords within your site's meta tags. When you design a web page, you use meta tags to provide structured information about it. Meta tags are part of the computer language called HTML which makes up the pages you see on a website. Meta tags include the Title, Description, and Keyword tags.

Continuing with the football tips example, you could put "Five Football Tips to Improve Your Game" in between the title tags, place the description "Impress your coach and your team mates by copying the techniques of professional football players" between the description tags, and the key phrases "football tips, football techniques" within the keyword tags.

If you are using Wordpress, download the plugin All in One SEO Pack and enter the information in the meta tags located below the text box where you would type a new post or a new page.

All in One SEO Pack

Upgrade to All in One SEO Pack Pro Version

Five Football Tips to Improve Your Game

Title: 39 characters. Most search engines use a maximum of 60 chars for the title.

Impress your coach and your team mates by copying the techniques of professional football players.

Description: 98 characters. Most search engines use a maximum of 160 chars for the description.

Keywords (comma separated): football tips, football techniques

Disable on this page/post: ☐

Step 3: Include your keywords in the body title of your web page. When you write an article, for example, the heading should be bolder and larger than the rest of the content. This is the title of your article.

Step 4: Use your keywords multiple times within your content. Don't overdo it. You cannot fool the search engines by using certain keywords repeatedly in your content. For example, you could use the key phrase "learn to play basketball" at least two or three times within your content. The phrase could appear once in each paragraph.

Step 5: Create a hyperlink of your keywords. The phrase "football tips" could be changed into an active hyperlink that a viewer could click on, which would lead to a different page containing a list of football tips or an index of articles.

Step 6: Place your keywords in the "ALT" tag with your image. When you upload an image on your Wordpress site, be sure to type in your keywords with your image. You could have a picture of someone about to kick a ball and you could include your keywords "football tips".

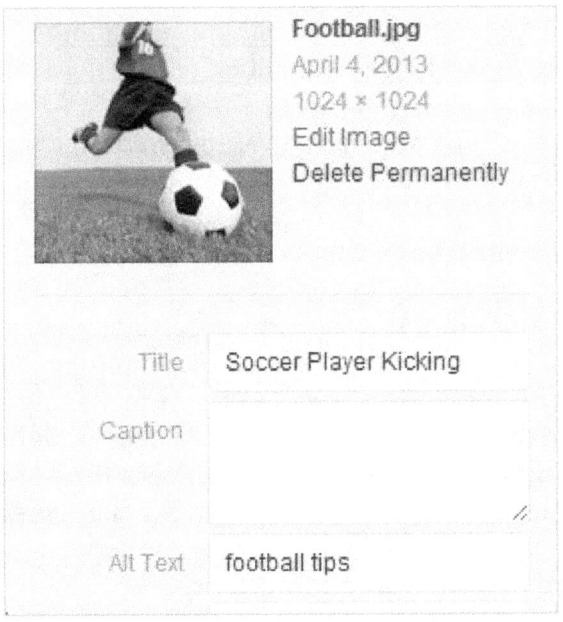

These are just the first few steps you can take to optimize your site for the major search engines.

Submit Your Site to Search Engines

The most popular search engines are Yahoo, Google, and Bing. In order to submit your site to these top search engines you first need to create an email account with all of them. They all provide webmaster tools to advise you on how to optimize your site and they also give recommendations and guidelines on the design, content, and quality of your site. Click on the following links to begin your site submission:

Google
http://www.google.com/submityourcontent/website-owner
Yahoo http://search.yahoo.com/info/submit.html
Binghttp://www.bing.com/toolbox/webmaster

(Yahoo and Bing both have the same web page where you submit your site.)

Submit Your Content to Article Directories

A great way to attract long term targeted customers to your site is by writing an article and submitting it to article directories. This is called article marketing and this is one of the tools you should include in your online marketing strategy. Article marketing is a form of internet advertising in which online businesses write short articles about themselves and their products and services online and submit them to article directories.

To begin marketing your articles, first write at least 5 to 10 keyword rich articles, or hire someone to do it for you (e.g. a ghost writer). When writing your articles, make sure that you optimize each article with relevant keywords which relate to the product you are promoting. You can optimize your article by placing keywords into the title of the article, integrating two or three keywords into the body of your article, and by using your keywords in anchor text in your external links.

For example, if your keyword was 'losing weight' then your article title would be "Top 10 Ways to Lose Weight" with 'lose weight' being the keyword you are using to optimize your article content. In the body of your article you could integrate keywords such as losing weight, weight loss techniques, and weight loss programs. And your anchor text would read http://www.weightlosstechniques.com.

Once you have written a few articles you can then submit them to the various article directories. Here is a list of article directories that you can check out:

Ezine Articles http://www.ezinearticles.com
Go Articles http://www.goarticles.com
Articles Base http://www.articlesbase.com
Article Alley http://www.articlealley.com
Ideal Marketers http://www.idealmarketers.com
Search Warp http://searchwarp.com
Buzzle http://www.buzzle.com
Amazineshttp://www.amazines.com
Web Source http://www.web-source.net

You can submit your articles manually or by using free article submission software called Article Submission Helper (http://www.articlesubmissionhelper.com). Article Submission Helper is a free article submission tool that helps you to submit your article to multiple article directories.

Place an Ad on Free Classified Ads Sites

If you have your own product or service to sell, then submitting an advertisement to free classified ads sites is the way to go. Free classifieds advertising is one of the most powerful online advertising tools on the web. You can submit your ad to thousands of free classified ads sites and reach millions of web users. There are many people on the web who will be willing to buy your product.

Classifieds advertising is free of cost, which saves your business a lot of money; you can reach your targeted audience within your local area and it saves you time for your business promotion. Additionally, you can get free traffic to your website or blog with free classifieds advertising. You can add a link to your website with your advertisement so you get direct traffic to your site without spending any money. You could start selling your products within a few days.

When writing your ad, make sure that it grabs the attention of the reader. Always place relevant keywords in the title and body of your ad. Also ensure that your classified ad is compelling and that it encourages people to click the link to your website so that they may read more about what you have to offer.

Once you have completed your ad, and are sure that it is an attention grabber, make sure to choose the right category where you want to position your ad. For example, if you wanted to advertise discounts on hotel stays then you would place your ad in the Travel Getaway category of classified ads sites. The headline of your ad should also have the main benefit of the product you are promoting clearly featured.

When posting your ad to the various classified ads sites, always remember that you don't have to include your phone number or address. You should provide a direct link to your website instead.

It only takes a couple of minutes to post your ad. It goes live immediately and is available to website visitors. You can post as many classified ads as you want to. There is no limit.

Check out these free classified ads sites:

Internet Marketer http://www.internetmarketer.com
Gumtree http://www.gumtree.com
Qype http://www.qype.co.uk
Craig's List http://www.craigslist.com
Adlandpro http://www.adlandpro.com
Adpost http://www.adpost.com
Classifieds http://www.classifieds.co.uk
Free Ads http://www.freeads.co.uk
Backpage http://www.backpage.com
Inetgiant http://www.inetgiant.com

Email Marketing

Email marketing is direct marketing in which an organization sends a commercial message to a group of people using electronic mail, or email for short. Every email you send to a potential or existing customer is considered email marketing. You can use email to send advertisements, solicit sales or donations, request business, or persuade people to subscribe to your newsletter.

One type of email marketing that you should include in your online advertising campaign is opt-in email advertising. Also referred to as permission marketing, opt-in email advertising is a method of online advertising via email in which the recipient of the advertisement has consented to receive it.

For example, a company may send a newsletter via email to its customers. These newsletters are used to inform customers of upcoming events, promotions, or new products. In permission marketing, a business that wants to email a newsletter to its customers may ask them at the point of purchase if they want to receive the newsletter.

You want to email as many potential customers as possible, but you don't want your email to be considered spam and deleted automatically from the user's inbox. In order to send commercial email, there are a few guidelines that you must follow such as:

1. You must include a return email address in your email messages.
2. You must include a valid physical address of your business.
3. Provide a one-click unsubscribe feature in the email.

4. Prohibit importing lists of purchased addresses that may not have given valid permission.

To start email marketing, one of the tools you will need is a good autoresponder. If you are using Wordpress then you can find a free and easy to use autoresponder plugin such as WP Autoresponder and Newsletter Plugin. On the other hand, if you would prefer to use a service other than the Wordpress plugin, then I would suggest Aweber. This is a great marketing tool to build your email list with and it is easy to use.

Next create your email lists. You can start with two: New customers and existing customers.

Third, build your email list. This can be done in the following ways:

1. Offer something of value for free on your website in exchange for the person's email address.
2. Add an email sign-up form on your Facebook page.
3. Ask for the person's email address when they enquire about your product or service in person or on the phone.
4. Create a system to obtain the person's email address during the order process.
5. Ask your family and friends for their email addresses.
6. Include a sign-up form on your website.

When you have built up your email list, make sure that you write content that your target audience wants to read. Your content should be interesting and informative. Your content should also include actionable steps that your readers can take to meet their needs which inspired them to read your publication in the first place. Writing high-quality content builds trust among your readers and leads to both purchases and word-of-mouth marketing.

Your email marketing campaign will not be very successful if you don't have a good email autoresponder. You can use autoresponders to follow up with your customers and generate sales repeatedly while you are sleeping or on vacation.

It takes only three simple steps to use an autoresponder. First, load all the email addresses you collected into the autoresponder program or website. Second, write a series of emails to those customers, that is, your email list. And third, schedule those emails to be sent automatically at a future date.

Video Marketing

Online video marketing is a great way for you to spread the message about your website to the online community. You can use video to promote your online business, your products and services, as well as your website. One of the ways to get viewers to watch your video is by submitting it to YouTube.com and other video sites.

You don't need any expensive technical equipment or software to create a video. You don't even need to hire a camera crew. All you really need is a webcam, your smart phone, digital or video camera, a microphone, and free video editing software, such as Windows Movie

Maker which comes with your Windows operating system (XP, Vista, Windows 7, or higher).

If you want to create videos using your computer, such as making an onscreen video on how to use particular software, then you can use video recording software such as Camstudio, Camtasia, or Animoto. You can use any of the software mentioned and see which one you like the best.

When you have completed your video, go to YouTube.com and sign up for a free account. Follow the instructions for submitting and uploading your video and that's all there is to it.

More and more businesses are promoting their products and services using creative videos and submitting them to YouTube. You can use online video marketing to grow your internet business and attract customers to your site. There are many advantages to using videos to generate targeted traffic to your site, such as:

1. Online users tend to click on video ads more than image or text ads which increase the chance that your video ad will be viewed more by online users than other types of ads.
2. Video marketing can help you to stand out from your competitors by creating videos that present your business in a different way.
3. Using online videos encourages visitors to stay on your website longer, which allows businesses to generate sales.
4. Online videos are a great way to grab a person's attention, instead of having them read paragraphs

upon paragraphs of text. Some visitors prefer to listen and watch a video than read text. This gives you the perfect opportunity to pitch your product or service in a 60 second video.

5. Networking is becoming more essential to internet marketing these days. Videos are being shared online all the time. You can submit a video to YouTube.com and share it on Facebook, MySpace, Twitter and other social networking sites. Before you know it, millions of people all over the world have seen your video.

6. By creating a video and submitting it online, you can increase click through rates to your website and show visitors different aspects of your online business.

7. Submitting your video to YouTube.com can increase your search engine ranking and drive more online traffic to your site.

There are many different ways you can use videos online. The following are examples of how you can use online videos:

1. Create a video of each product you're selling, how it works, and how other people are using it.

2. Record your customers' testimonials on video and share them on your website or through social networking sites like YouTube, Facebook, and Twitter.

3. Make a video giving an overview of your company, its key messages, and a brief description of your products and services. You can place this video on your About Us page.

4. Create and display videos advertising your products and services on various websites and social networking sites.
5. Give a demonstration of how to assemble your product and how it works. Include a user manual.
6. You can make a video of your case studies, including a text format of the case study. In your video you can show visitors how your business has benefited others, what approach you took and what was the final outcome.
7. You can record live interviews with experts in your chosen niche, your customers, your suppliers, or share your success stories. You can share these interviews on YouTube as well as on your website.
8. Save time and money by creating an online training video. This is beneficial to your customers and students in that they can access the training video in their own time and work with it at their own pace.

In order for people to find your video, you have to perform the same tasks that you did for article marketing and creating classified ads: you need to do your keyword research. Use the Google Keyword Tool to find out what people are searching for. Look for keywords that are relevant to the product you are promoting and implement them into the title of your video.

When you upload your video, include video tags so that it can be found by people who are searching for what your video shows. Place at least 15 tags for your video so that it will be returned as a related video for as many searches as possible.

Your video should also have a long description of what it is about. Your description should contain relevant keywords as well to let people know that your content is useful and helpful. And don't forget to include a link to your website which you can put at the top of the video description.

You can upload your video to the following video sites:

You Tube http://www.youtube.com
Vimeo http://vimeo.com
Yahoo Video http://video.yahoo.com
Daily Motion http://www.dailymotion.com

Presently many people are spending more time online and are getting used to watching videos on the internet. As you are starting your online business, take advantage of this great opportunity and create an online video to reach your target audience. This is a great way to grab the attention of online users and generate sales.

Write a Press Release

Another way to market your business online is by writing or recording a press release and submitting it to the various PR websites. A press release is a written or recorded communication distributed to the news media for the purpose of announcing the opening of a new business, the launching of a new product or service, or the venue of a special event. A press release should contain information that is useful, accurate, and interesting.

Many press release websites have established a particular format that you must follow when writing and submitting a press release. The following are a few guidelines:

1. Press releases should be printed on the company letterhead with the company logo. The company's name, web address, physical address, email address and phone number should be printed clearly at the top of the page.

2. PRESS RELEASE should be typed out in capital letters and centred in bold. The press release contact person's name and contact numbers should be printed clearly underneath the bold title. If the press release is for IMMEDIATE RELEASE then type it out on the left margin directly above the title in capital letters.

3. The headline or title of the press release should be bold and centred. The title should be short and snappy, grabbing the attention of the reader, impressing them enough to continue reading the press release.

4. Begin the content, or body of the press release with the date and city from which the press release is originated. The body of the press release should contain answers to the questions: Who, what, where, when, and why. The first paragraph should give brief details as to what the press release is about.

5. The second paragraph is more informative and explains in detail who cares, why you should care, where one can find it, and when it will happen. You should also include a quote which gives the press release a personal touch.

6. The third and final paragraph is where you summarize the press release and give further information about your company with the company contact information included.

7. The content of the press release, starting with the date and city of origin, should be typed in a clear basic font such as Times New Roman or Arial, and double spaced.

8. If your press release has more than one page, then the second page should indicate 'Page Two' in the upper right hand corner. At the end of the press release place three symbols (###), without the brackets, in the centre directly underneath the last line of the release.

Below is an example of how a press release should be formatted:

Anywhere Technologies

121 Boardwalk, Any Town, Any City, UK, AB1 9YZ
Website: www.anytech.com Email: info@anytech.com

IMMEDIATE RELEASE

PRESS RELEASE
MISS JANE DOE
TEL: (44) 000 000 0000
MOBILE: (44) 000 000 0000

[Headline/Title]

[Date] April 4, 2012

[City of Origin of Press Release] London, UK

First Paragraph: Details as to what the press release is about, such as who, what, where, when, why, and how?

Second Paragraph: Who cares? Why should you care? Where can one find it? When will it happen? [Include a quote]

Third Paragraph: Summarize the press release. Give further information about your company. Include company contact information.

###

Once you have completed your press release, you can then submit it to the following press release sites:

PR Free http://www.prfree.com
SB Wire http://www.sbwire.com
PR http://www.pr.com
i-News Wire http://www.i-newswire.com
eReleaseshttp://www.ereleases.com
Web Wire http://www.webwire.com
Free Press Release http://www.free-press-release.com
PR Web http://www.prweb.com

Join Online Forums

Your business can benefit from joining online forums in many ways. An online forum, also known as a message board, is an online discussion site where people can join and converse with one another in the form of posted messages. In some forums a posted message may need to be approved by a moderator before it becomes visible for others to read and respond to.

Forums can contain several sub-forums in which each one may have a different topic. When a new topic is introduced into a forum, a new discussion is started which is called a 'thread'. Each thread can be replied to by as many people as is allowed.

As mentioned above, there are many benefits to joining online forums. You can even start your own forum, or community, in which you can build a relationship with your customers. For example, you could join a forum in your niche to find out what sort of products and services people are using and how they feel about it. This is a great way to do some market research when creating a new product.

Another benefit of online forums is that they allow you to communicate with your potential customers through social networking. These forums or communities give consumers the opportunity to talk to one another and ask questions about different products and services. It is now possible for you as a business owner to foster relationships and gain insight into your customers through conversations with them.

Furthermore, online forums can help you to drive more traffic to your site. Active forums are usually indexed by Google and all the other search engines. So if you join an active forum and post regularly to these forums then you will be sure to attract more traffic to your site through the search engines.

The following are useful guidelines that you should take note of when joining an online forum:

1. Before joining a forum, make sure that you are allowed to include a signature document. This 'sig' document will appear below each of your posts each time you publish. When creating your signature include a brief summary of yourself, your online business and include a link back to

your website. Although you may be limited to writing 3 or 4 lines, you should at least make the short description of your business and your website so interesting that forum readers will want to visit your site to find out more what it is about.

2. Be sure to create a complete profile of yourself. The information you include in your profile will help give authority and trust that your responses or new threads you create are coming from a great expert in your niche.

3. You should only join forums that are related to your online business. If you want to attract the right kind of traffic to your site, then you need to join forums that are in your niche.

4. Don't just send a post in any thread – instead look for those that have the most activity, for example, the principal discussion thread. Even before you publish a single post, take the time to study the discussion threads, the rules, and the types of threads being created. You can use this time to collect information which can help you to create interesting posts and good responses to the other members of the forum.

5. You could start a discussion with a popular topic that is of particular interest to forum readers. This should result in a lot of action or responses to your post.

6. Make an effort to post some interesting bits of information at least a few times a week. It doesn't have to be every day.

7. Provide relevant and helpful information in response to individual threads. You can gain the respect of the other forum readers and the forum could identify you as an expert within that particular niche.

8. One way you can ensure that your posts get read is by optimizing them with the appropriate keywords or key phrases so that your posts will get a high ranking in the search engines.

9. You can also use online forums to come up with ideas for articles to post on your blog. Just keep track of the threads that are generating a great deal of discussion.

Online forums are a great way to market your online business on the internet for free. It may take a little time and some effort but the rewards for your 'labour' are fairly significant. You don't have to join a lot of forums – 2 or 3 forums are enough, which you can add to your internet marketing campaign.

To find forums in your particular niche, you can search through the following sites:

Pro Boards http://www.proboards.com
Zeta Boards http://www.zetaboards.com
Forum Finder http://www.theforumfinder.com
Forum Doc http://www.forumdr.com

Create Slideshows

You can use the articles you wrote to convert them into simple slideshows to pre-sell the product you are promoting or your website. Your slideshows don't have to be long, but they should at least grab and retain the reader's interest and attention and to direct them to your website.

When creating your slideshow you must ensure that you break up the text into 2 – 3 line sentences so that it will be easy to read. As always, make sure that you include tags and keywords so that your slideshows appear whenever someone does a search on the website using your chosen keywords.

You can submit your slideshow presentations to the following sites:

http://www.Scribd.com
http://www.slideshare.net
http://www.4shared.com

Promote Your Affiliate Links or Your Website with PLR Content

If all this sounds new to you, PLR stands for Private Label Rights content which you can purchase and integrate your link to your website into the content. These could be e-books, articles or reports and you can distribute them through your blog, website or submit them to e-book directories and forums.

Once you purchase a PLR e-book or report, open the document for editing in your word processor, such as Microsoft Word. You may want to spend some time reading through the material to ensure that there are no spelling or grammatical mistakes, and also to ensure that the material contains up-to-date information.

You could also rewrite the Table of Contents, maybe even adjust the title of the e-book. And don't forget to insert your name as the author of the e-book and include your affiliate links. Ensure that the link to your website is displayed at the beginning, middle and end of the document.

Then convert your document into PDF format and make sure that your links are still clickable. To create a PDF, simply click on Save As, and select PDF in the drop down menu next to 'Save as Type'. If you are having trouble converting your document to PDF then you can upload your Word document to http://www.freepdfconvert.com.

You can find great PLR content at the following sites:

http://www.superplr.com
http://www.plr365.com
http://www.ebooks-land.com
http://www.wealthandfreedompackage.com

Once you have completed your e-book or report you can upload your content to free e-book directory sites such as:

http://www.tradebit.com

http://www.scribd.com
http://ebookdirectory.com
http://www.ebookslibrary.com
http://www.free-ebooks.net
http://www.upload.com

Market Your Site on Social Networks

Just by spending a few minutes each day on social networks, like Facebook and Twitter, can make all the difference in generating a large volume of free traffic quickly and easily.

However, you need to be as active as possible and post a combination of free and informative messages on social networks. You can also post promotional messages as well with a direct link to your website or an affiliate link to the merchant's website.

You may be more successful in generating a response by sending people to your website which contains useful, important or entertaining information with your affiliate links already embedded into the content, rather than posting an affiliate link to the social community.

Before sending out messages that offer free downloads and links to your website or the merchant's page, you should at least post a few short entertaining messages and useful tips in order to warm up your audience. Then after a few days, you can start posting free downloads, such as your PLR contents to your followers and the social community without directly selling to them.

Posting messages to the social community can be very time consuming, but it is well worth the effort when you succeed in promoting your website and affiliate products to your target audience.

The following is a list of popular social communities that you can join for free:

Facebook http://www.facebook.com
Twitter http://www.twitter.com
Linked In http://www.linkedin.com

Create a Facebook Fan Page to Drive Traffic to Your Site

Facebook is one of the most popular social network sites on the internet which I highly recommend that you join right away if you want to gain mass exposure for your site. You can create an account on Facebook for free and then set up your profile page and Facebook fan page.

You should create a Facebook fan page because it gives you the opportunity to promote your products and your website for free, it allows you to build a reputation as an expert in your chosen niche market, you can grow your commissions through massive exposure on Facebook, and by using your fan page you can drive a lot of traffic to your site. You can also promote your affiliate products on your fan page as well without exposing yourself as an affiliate.

To create your Facebook fan page go to http://www.facebook.com. If you do not have an account then enter your name, email address, password, date of birth, and select whether you are a male or female, and then click Sign Up. Once you have set up your account, then you go to the next step, which is to create your fan page.

Sign in to Facebook and click Create a Page on the left sidebar of your page. Then follow the instructions to create your fan page. Make sure that you upload a photo and include your website URL on your fan page. And as with all the other marketing techniques that I mentioned in this chapter, always use your best keywords to create a description for your fan page.

Once you have completed your Facebook fan page, you can invite your friends who are already on Facebook and those from your email address book to become fans of the page you just created. You can use your fan page to post daily or weekly updates of information and products you are offering on your website. You can include links to your affiliate products and links to useful information and free resources.

You can use the other popular social networks, likeLinkedin and Twitter to build your profile and interact with other potential customers.

Market Your Site Offline

Just because you plan to operate a business on the internet does not mean that you should neglect marketing your business offline. Traditional marketing methods can still be just as useful and effective in attracting people to your site and purchasing your products and services. As long as you've got the budget and the commitment to growing a successful online business, then it would be wise to utilize both methods.

The following traditional marketing methods can be used to promote your online business:

Business Cards

You already know what a business card is. A business card is a small rectangular card that has a person's information printed on it. A good business card should contain the following:

Your name
Your business title
Name of the company you own or work for
Company logo
Business telephone numbers
Business address
Email address and website URL
A brief description of your products/services and about you

A business card is a great marketing tool because it shows that you are a professional and that your company means business. It is also a great way to spread the news about your business through word of mouth. This form of marketing is a very effective method of making your potential customers aware of your business for almost no effort at all.

It is very easy to distribute business cards. One way you could distribute your business cards is by offering them in your work office to customers. You could place business cards in local libraries, restaurants, and markets. It is also a good idea to attend business seminars and workshops in which you introduce yourself with your business card.

Make sure that you include your website URL and your online business will be sure to grow.

Newspaper Advertising

Despite the growing preference of internet marketing, newspaper advertising can still produce positive results. Newspapers are distributed to large diverse audiences so they can be very effective when trying to raise awareness of your online business.

If you have the budget for it, you can place small advertisements in the newspaper for about a week. Try to have your ad placed in an area where editorial content will be wrapped around it. Also ensure that your ad is positioned on the right hand side of the page where more people will see it.

Chapter 8: Planning and Registering Your Online Business

If you are serious about starting an online business and generating revenue on the internet, then you should consider writing a business plan and registering your business. But don't quit your day job just yet. Once you have registered your business you need to ensure that you can make a steady income online before quitting your job. But there are some things you need to understand first before registering your business, such as the legal structure you should choose, whether or not you need a business plan, coming up with a name for your business, and how to register your business. This section will cover all of the essentials for planning and registering your online business.

Which Legal Structure is Right for Your Business?

You need to think carefully about the way you intend to do business and which legal structure suits you the best. The legal structure you choose will affect the following:

1. The authorities you have to inform of the existence of your business
2. Taxes and National Insurance that you have to pay
3. The financial records that you have to keep
4. Your financial liability if your business encounters financial challenges
5. The way you raise funds for your business

6. The way management decisions are made about running the business

Since you are starting up a small business, there are two legal structures that you can choose from: a Sole Trader or a Partnership. There are other legal structures such as a Limited Liability company and a Corporation, but these are beyond the scope of this book.

Registering as a Sole Trader

A sole trader is a business that is formed by one individual who is considered to be the owner. Becoming a sole trader, or self-employed, is the simplest way of starting a business. This is because all of the profits earned by the business belong to one person, that is, the owner. Other characteristics of a sole trader include:

1. You do not have to pay any registration fees to become a sole trader.
2. Keeping records and accounts is straightforward.
3. You get to keep all of the profits your business generates.
4. You make all of the decisions on how to run your business.
5. You raise money for your business using your own assets or with a loan.
6. You are personally liable for any debts your business incurs.
7. You have to pay tax and national insurance.

Registering as a Partnership

A partnership is another type of legal business structure in which two or more individuals join together as co-owners of a business for profit. The capital required to organize the business is raised by each partner making a financial contribution. The features of a partnership are as follows:

1. Partners share the risks, costs and responsibilities of being in business.
2. A partner can be an individual or another business.
3. Profits and gains of the partnership are shared among the partners, unless stated otherwise in the partnership agreement.
4. Each partner is responsible for paying tax on their share of the profits and national contribution.
5. Each partner must register for self-assessment with HM Revenue & Customs (HMRC) and complete an annual tax return.
6. A nominated partner must send HMRC a partnership return.
7. Partners use their own assets or loans to raise capital for the business.
8. The partners themselves usually manage the business, but they can delegate certain responsibilities to employees.
9. It is possible that a partnership can have "sleeping partners", i.e. those who make financial contributions to the business but are not involved in the day to day operations.
10. The partnership must keep financial records of income generated and expenses incurred by the business.

To avoid any misunderstandings and legal battles in court, it is always wise to draw up a written agreement between the partners.

If you are unsure of which business structure is suitable for your business, then it is highly recommended that you seek professional advice from an accountant or a solicitor.

How do You Come Up with a Business Name?

Now that you have thought carefully and chosen a legal structure that is suitable for your business, the next step is to come up with a good name for your business. Besides deciding on a legal structure, choosing a proper name is one of the most important steps when starting your online business. Whether you have a bricks-and-mortar business or one that is operated completely on the internet, your business name has to be effective because it is the first thing that people will see and you want it to create a good impression. Therefore it is essential that you come up with the best name for your business.

The following tips will give you some ideas for coming up with a good business name.

Your business name should appeal to your target market. Think of the kind of people you want to sell to or do business with and check if the business name you come up with will appeal to them. For example, *Tiny Tots Nursery* uses the name 'tiny tots' to describe children who are between the ages of 1 and 2 years.

Your business name can describe what you do. For example, *John's Taxi & Tour Services* is a simple and straightforward business name that tells people that the business offers taxi and island tour services.

Ensure that your business name is short, easy to pronounce, spell and remember. Keep it simple. Don't use tongue twisters and unfamiliar words.

Don't use trendy names. In other words, don't name your business after popular television shows. As you already know, television shows run for a certain period of time and are then taken off the air. So if you do not want your business to have a stale and outdated name like so many television programs, then avoid using trendy names.

Write a Good Business Plan

When starting a business, whether a physical company or an online enterprise, it is always a good idea to write a business plan. It doesn't have to be long and complicated. It could be a simple document about two or three pages long. A business plan is simply a document which describes what your business does, where it is going, and what resources are required to get there.

Every business should have a business plan and it should be updated on an annual basis as your business grows. Don't think that the only time you need a business plan is when you are applying for a loan. There are other reasons why you should write a business plan.

Why Should You Write a Business Plan?

You should write a business plan if you are going to start and run a business. Writing a business plan helps you to focus on your objectives and how you plan to accomplish those objectives, it helps you to determine whether your idea is a profitable one, and it forces you to examine the financial side of operating a business.

If you need funding from a financial institution, then it is imperative that you write a business plan. Any bank you go to will expect you to have prepared a business plan.

Are you looking for people to invest in your business? Then you need to write a business plan. The business plan does not guarantee that you will get the investment, but no investor will take you seriously if you don't present a business plan. Investors need to know what your business does and how it will make money, thus the reason why you should write a business plan.

Furthermore, if you plan on taking on partners to contribute to the development of your business, then you will need to write a business plan with them in mind. When writing your business plan, you need to include agreements between partners about what's going to happen with your company and what each of them will be responsible for.

If you intend to sell your business, then you will need to write a business plan. You need to set a value on the business for tax or other purposes such as estate planning or divorce.

Developing a business plan is much easier than you think. In order to be successful you need to plan what steps you are going to take to get started, determine what resources are required for your business, and how you will manage your company's cash flow.

The information you include in your business plan should be based on the type of business you have. But the main components you should include in your business plan, should you decide to create one, are the following:

Executive Summary – Although it comes at the beginning of your business plan, this section should be written last. It is an overall description of your business.

Company Description – This section contains the basic details of your company such as its legal structure, history if it is an existing business, start up plans if it is new, location, what segment of the market the business is targeting, etc.

Management Team – Include all the information regarding the management of the company. Give names, job titles, description of the roles of each manager, etc.

Product or Service – Describe the various products and services you offer and how you offer it to your target market.

Market Analysis – In this section you need to describe every relevant aspect of the market in which you will market your product or service.

Strategy and Implementation – Explain how you will attract and maintain your customer base.

Financial Plan – This is the most difficult part of the business plan. Include financial projections of your business such as cash flow, balance sheet, and income statements.

Executive Summary

The executive summary may be the most important section in your business plan. The contents of your executive summary will determine whether your readers continue reading or cast it aside to read something more interesting. You need to write an executive summary that will compel your readers to delve into your business plan to read more about your idea. The executive summary is an overall picture of your business; therefore you should give a brief description of the main aspects of your business such as the following:

1. The name of your business and whether it is brand new or an ongoing organization
2. Include the objectives of your business. You could do this using bullet points.
3. When the timeline of your business plan will go into effect
4. Give a brief description of your product/service and how it will interact with your target market.
5. In the next paragraph, summarize the business plan's intended market, industry and market segment you are targeting. Ensure that your reader understands what sort of customer you will be focusing your marketing efforts on.

6. The third paragraph could be a brief description of the core skills and experience of each person on your management team, if there's any, and how they will contribute to the implementation of your business plan.
7. Next, discuss the strategy, implementation and marketing plans of your business.
8. Include the keys to success to show your readers the strengths of your business. For example, you could list what your business will bring to your target market.
9. And in the final paragraph, state the intention or purpose of your plan. If you are writing a business plan because you want to apply for a loan, for example, then you can include the total amount your business requires and the repayment details.

Company Description

This is a very important component of your plan in that your readers will want to know more about your business. In this section, you need to include basic details of your company such as history (if your business already exists) or a start-up summary listing the resources or business expenses you will incur when you start your business. You should also include the following in your company description:

1. The name and location of your business
2. The legal structure of your business
3. A mention of your products and services
4. What segment of the market your company will target

5. Ensure that you add an effective mission statement in your company description.

How to Write an Effective Mission Statement

Your mission statement is an opportunity for you to tell people what your business is about in three or four sentences or less. The most essential points you need to include in your mission statement are: Who your company is, what does your company do, what do you believe in, what your values are, and why does your company do what it is doing now?

In your mission statement, you could also address the following:

1. How much profit you want to make
2. Who is your target market?
3. What benefits do you offer the market you are serving?
4. What problem you solve for your customers
5. What kind of work environment you want for your employees?

Keep your mission statement short and simple. Make sure that your mission statement is about you, your company and your ideals. Although it is a good idea to look at examples of mission statements, try not to copy them. Your mission statement should be original and unique.

Management Team

It is important to include the management team summary when writing your business plan. In this section you should include all the relevant information that pertains to your management team such as:

1. Names and job titles of each manager
2. A brief description of their skills and experience
3. Management personnel that will be added to the company at a later date
4. Managers' compensation rates
5. Identify any consultants the company plans to hire
6. Management structure

You could start your management team summary by giving a brief explanation about your management team. Include how many employees your company has, how many managers, and if any of the managers are founders or partners.

You may not think that this section applies to you because you are self-employed and you won't be hiring anyone to work with you, but you still need to write this section. You could at least write about yourself and your qualifications and experience.

Product or Service

No business plan is complete without a description of the products and services you intend to sell. When describing your offering, make sure that you cover the main points such as:

1. What the product or service is
2. What it does (i.e. what problem does it solve?)
3. How much it costs
4. What kind of customer would be interested in purchasing this product or service, and why?

If you have many products or services that you plan to sell, there is no need to list all of them. You could focus on the main products that you plan to offer your target market.

When describing your product or service, always keep the customer you plan to serve in mind. Think of their needs and benefits and how you plan to fulfil their desires.

Market Analysis

This is the part where you examine your primary target market for your product or service such as geographic location, demographics, your target market's needs and how these needs are being met currently. You should start your market analysis by first segmenting the market and then identifying your target market.

Market segmentation involves dividing large diverse markets into smaller segments that can be reached more efficiently and effectively with products and services that match their unique needs. There are four ways you can segment a market: geographic, demographic, psychographic, and behavioural.

Geographic segmentation involves dividing the market into different geographical units such as nations, regions, states, countries, cities, or neighbourhoods. For example, if you are starting a plumbing business, then you would segment the market by neighbourhood or by city.

Using demographic segmentation, you may divide the market into groups based on age, gender, family size, income, occupation, education, religion, race or nationality.

Psychographic segmentation involves dividing consumers into different groups based on social class, lifestyle, or personality characteristics.

Behavioural segmentation divides consumers into groups based on their knowledge, attitudes, uses, or responses to a product. This may be the best way to begin building market segments.

After evaluating different segments, you now need to decide which and how many segments you will target. A target market is a set of buyers that share common needs or characteristics that you choose to supply your offerings to.

The best form of marketing for an online business that has limited resources is concentrated or niche marketing. This is a market-coverage strategy in which you target a large share of one or a few segments or niches. The advantage of niche marketing is that you are concentrating on a smaller segment which attracts only a few competitors, unlike larger segments.

The next thing you need to do is to identify and understand your main competitors. Find out what products or services they offer, their strengths and weaknesses, whether they operate their business online, offline or both, how they get their products into the hands of consumers, and try to find out how their customers feel about their products and services.

Strategy and Implementation

After you have segmented the market, identified your target audience and studied your competitors, the next thing you need to do is come up with a good marketing strategy and how it will be implemented into your business. This calls for using the four P's of the marketing mix. To put it simply, the marketing mix consists of four marketing tools that you will use to create demand for your products and services. The four P's of the marketing mix are Product, Price, Place (Distribution) and Promotion.

Product is the good or service that you offer to your target market. Price is the amount of money customers agree to pay to obtain your product. Place involves all the distribution channels that you use to make the product available to your target consumers. Promotion includes activities that communicate the benefits derived from using the product and persuade customers to buy it.

For example, let's say that you wanted to sell a car. The engine, tires, headlights, wind shield, spark plugs, etc. make up the product, that is, your car. Next, in order to set a price for your car, you would examine the prices your competitors may charge for their cars. You may set your price higher or lower than what your competitors are charging. The price would also be determined based on your expenses in maintaining and servicing the car.

The next step is to determine the place where you will sell your car, that is, the distribution channels. You could arrange to have the car displayed at a garage, or from your home, or at a used car dealership. And finally, you need to promote your car. You could place an ad in a local newspaper or on a classified ads site on the internet. You could also hand out flyers or have your advertisement aired on the radio.

When you have come up with your marketing strategy, you then need to determine how you will implement it into your business. There are two ways you could implement your marketing strategy. One way is to do it yourself or to get your employees to do it for you. The other way is to hire a marketing firm or ad agency to implement your marketing strategy. It is always better to perform the marketing strategy yourself to avoid the high cost of hiring external firms.

Website Development and Marketing Strategy

Since you plan on building a website, you need to have a proper website marketing strategy. First you need to come up with a domain name using relevant keywords, purchase web hosting, design the website, and market it on the internet. You need to determine whether you will be designing the website yourself or if you are going to hire a professional to do it for you.

Additionally, you need to determine how you are going to update and maintain the website as well. This is why it is better to build the website yourself so that you will be able to maintain it and keep it up to date, rather than build up recurring expenses in hiring a professional to do the job.

You also need to include in your business plan how you plan to market your website. This can be done through article marketing, email marketing, banner advertising, exchanging links, joining online forums, submitting a video to video-sharing websites, joining social networking sites, and placing an advertisement on a free classified ads site.

Financial Plan

Your business plan is not complete without a solid financial plan. In the financial section of your business plan you should include important assumptions, sales forecast, projected cash flow, projected profit and loss, projected balance sheet, and break-even analysis.

Important Assumptions

You need to include important assumptions in your business plan. These assumptions are what you would use to calculate your projected financial statements. For example, your assumptions may be based on the seasonality of your products such as a hike in sales at Christmas time or on Valentine's Day. You may also assume your fixed costs for the year, the unit variable cost of your product and the unit selling price.

There are other factors which you must consider and include in your assumptions before calculating your financial projections. As a new online business, your sales assumptions need to be based on your market research and good judgment. The following factors should be considered when making your sales assumptions:

The Market – Examine the growth of the market you want to enter and whether your market share will grow or shrink. The increase or decrease of market share depends on the success or failure of your competitors.

Your Resources – If your online business is doing well, you may require increasing your sales force from 3 to 6 people. Or you may spend less money on advertising, which would have a negative impact on sales.

Overcoming Barriers to Sales – You may have found other distribution channels to sell your products such as through other affiliates or you placed banner ads on other websites which will increase sales. You may raise the prices of your products to increase revenue.

Your Products – Maybe you have new products coming out this year that have the potential to increase sales rapidly and have strong growth potential, or your sales may decline because your competitor's products are more superior.

Study these factors and apply them to your business plan when creating your sales forecast and other financial projections.

Sales Forecast

Developing your sales forecast is not as difficult as you may think. Your sales forecast is simply making an educated guess about how many product units will sell throughout the year. To create your sales forecast, first break down your sales to manageable parts, and then forecast the parts. You can break down your sales by product category, market or geographic region.

Your sales forecast is the starting point for financial projections, so it is important to use realistic estimates. You can start by dividing your projected monthly sales into product categories which are natural divisions that make sense for your type of business.

The following illustration is an example of a sales forecast of an online business that sold digital products, books and software from its website, which was done in Excel:

Fiscal Year Begins	Jan-13												
					12-Month Sales Forecast								
	Jan-13	Feb-13	Mar-13	Apr-13	May-13	Jun-13	Jul-13	Aug-13	Sep-13	Oct-13	Nov-13	Dec-13	Annual Totals
Printed Books	0	20	40	60	80	100	120	140	160	180	200	220	1320
Sale Price @ unit	50.00	50.00	50.00	50.00	50.00	50.00	50.00	50.00	50.00	50.00	50.00	50.00	
TOTAL	0	1,000	2,000	3,000	4,000	5,000	6,000	7,000	8,000	9,000	10,000	11,000	66,000
Software	100	150	200	250	300	350	400	450	500	550	600	650	4500
Sale Price @ unit	75.00	75.00	75.00	75.00	75.00	75.00	75.00	75.00	75.00	75.00	75.00	75.00	
TOTAL	7,500	11,250	15,000	18,750	22,500	26,250	30,000	33,750	37,500	41,250	45,000	48,750	337,500
E-Books	30	60	90	120	150	180	210	240	270	300	330	360	2340
Sale Price @ unit	25.00	25.00	25.00	25.00	25.00	25.00	25.00	25.00	25.00	25.00	25.00	25.00	
TOTAL	750	1,500	2,250	3,000	3,750	4,500	5,250	6,000	6,750	7,500	8,250	9,000	58,500
E-Courses	25	50	75	100	125	150	175	200	225	250	275	300	1950
Sale Price @ unit	250.00	250.00	250.00	250.00	250.00	250.00	250.00	250.00	250.00	250.00	250.00	250.00	
TOTAL	6,250	12,500	18,750	25,000	31,250	37,500	43,750	50,000	56,250	62,500	68,750	75,000	487,500
Advertising Space	0	0	5	10	15	20	25	30	35	40	45	50	275
See Price @ unit	100.00	100.00	100.00	100.00	100.00	100.00	100.00	100.00	100.00	100.00	100.00	100.00	
TOTAL	0	0	500	1,000	1,500	2,000	2,500	3,000	3,500	4,000	4,500	5,000	27,500
Monthly totals:	14,500	26,250	38,500	50,750	63,000	75,250	87,500	99,750	112,000	124,250	136,500	148,750	977,000

Projected Profit and Loss

As part of the financial section of your business plan, you need to include a profit and loss projection. The purpose of a profit and loss account is to determine whether your business has made either a profit or a loss during the financial year. It also describes how the profit or loss was incurred, for example, through categorizing costs between cost of sales and operating costs.

The profit and loss account begins with the trading account and then takes into account all the other expenses incurred by your business. The trading account shows the income generated from sales and the direct costs of making those sales. It includes the balance of stock at the beginning and end of the financial year.

Trading, Profit and Loss Projection

Category	£	£
Sales		977,000
Opening Stock	150,000	
Purchases	350,000	
Less Closing Stock	-100,000	
Cost of Sales	400,000	-400,000
Other Costs		-25,000
Gross Profit		552,000
Overheads or Expenses		
Rent	500	
Insurance	1,000	
Stationery & Postage	800	
Computer Maintenance	500	
Staff Salaries	24,000	
Sales & Marketing	5,000	
Advertising	2,000	
Bank Charges	500	
Total Expenses	34,300	-34,300
Net Profit		517,700
Taxation		-160,617
Net Profit After Tax		357,083

Take note that the Closing Stock figure in the Trading, Profit and Loss Projection would appear in the Balance Sheet under Stock.

Projected Cash Flow

The cash flow projection predicts the amount of net cash that flows into and out of your business over a future period of time. The cash flow forecast estimates what cash inflows and outflows from your business bank account will be. The result of the cash flow projection is an estimate of the bank balance at the end of each month covered.

The following is an example of a cash flow forecast done in Excel:

Cash Flow Forecast

	Jan	Feb	Mar	Apr	May	Jun
Cash at start of month	2,500	1,500	4,000	7,500	6,500	3,500
Cash inflows	2,000	5,000	7,000	4,000	2,500	1,500
Cash outflows	-3,000	2,500	3,500	-5,000	-5,500	-4,000
Net Cash Flow	-1,000	2,500	3,500	-1,000	-3,000	-2,500
Cash at end of month	1,500	4,000	7,500	6,500	3,500	1,000

Use the following formulae to calculate Net Cash Flow and Cash at the end of the month:

Step 1: Net Cash Flow = Cash Inflows – Cash Outflows
Step 2: Cash at the end of the Month = Cash at start of the month + Net Cash Flow

Take note that the cash at the end of the month is carried forward to the cash at the start of the following month. For example, the £1,500 was the cash at the end of the month of January. It was carried forward to the cash at the start of the month of February.

The cash flow forecast is a very important tool that all businesses should include in their business plan. Cash flow is the life blood of a business, especially start-ups and small enterprises. If your business runs out of cash and is unable to obtain more finance, then your business will die. Therefore it is essential that you predict what is going to happen to cash flow to make sure that your business has enough to survive.

Break-Even Analysis

The break-even analysis allows you to calculate what you will need to sell monthly or annually to cover the costs of doing business, that is, your break-even point. To calculate the break-even point, you need to know the following three assumptions:

Fixed Costs – These are costs that do not change even though production or sales levels change. Examples of fixed costs are rent, property tax, and insurance.

Variable Cost Per Unit – Variable cost is a cost related to production units. For example, direct materials and direct labor are variable costs. To calculate Total Variable Cost, multiply variable cost by the number of units sold. Add Total Variable Cost to Fixed Cost to get the Total Cost of production.

Selling Price Per Unit – This is the price that a unit is sold for. To calculate Total Sales, multiply the unit selling price by the number of units sold.

When Total Sales is equal to Total Costs, then we say that profits have reached the Break Even Point. The formula to use to calculate the Break Even Point is:

Break Even Point = Fixed Costs / (Unit Selling Price –
Unit Variable Cost)

Calculating the break-even point is the easy part, but
plotting a graph to show the break-even point is very
difficult. But I have produced the break-even point on a
graph and have worked out the calculations so that you
may see exactly how to do it.

The following illustration is an example of calculating the
Break Even Point in units as well as in cash, followed by
the Break Even graph:

Variable Cost Per Unit	£10 per unit
Selling Price Per Unit	£15 per unit
Fixed Costs	£2500 per month

Break Even Point (units) =   Fixed Costs / (Unit Selling
Price – Unit Variable Cost)

£2500 / (£15 - £10)
500

Break Even Point (£) =   500 x £15
£7500

Let us assume that for your first year in business you
expect your business to generate £15,000 (£15 x 1000
units) in total sales. And the total variable cost for the
year would be £10,000 (£10 x 1000).

Next, calculate Total Cost by multiplying the Variable
Cost per Unit (VCU) by the Number of Units and adding
the Fixed Cost (FC):

Total Cost = (VCU x Units) + FC

Now that you have this information you can arrange it all in tables and then plot your break-even graph. When creating the graph, do not forget to start the Sales Income from zero and begin the Variable Costs from the Fixed Costs line.

Example of Break-Even Analysis:

Break-Even Point

Break-Even: Toal Sales = Total Costs										
Number of Units	0	100	200	300	400	500	600	700	800	900	1,000
Variable Costs	10.00	10.00	10.00	10.00	10.00	10.00	10.00	10.00	10.00	10.00	10.00
Total Variable Cost	0	1,000	2,000	3,000	4,000	5,000	6,000	7,000	8,000	9,000	10,000
Number of Units	0	100	200	300	400	500	600	700	800	900	1,000
Selling Price	15.00	15.00	15.00	15.00	15.00	15.00	15.00	15.00	15.00	15.00	15.00
Total Sales	0	1,500	3,000	4,500	6,000	7,500	9,000	10,500	12,000	13,500	15,000
	0	100	200	300	400	500	600	700	800	900	1,000
Total Sales	0	1,500	3,000	4,500	6,000	7,500	9,000	10,500	12,000	13,500	15,000
Fixed Costs	2,500	2,500	2,500	2,500	2,500	2,500	2,500	2,500	2,500	2,500	2,500
Total Costs	2,500	3,500	4,500	5,500	6,500	7,500	8,500	9,500	10,500	11,500	12,500

Break-Even Chart

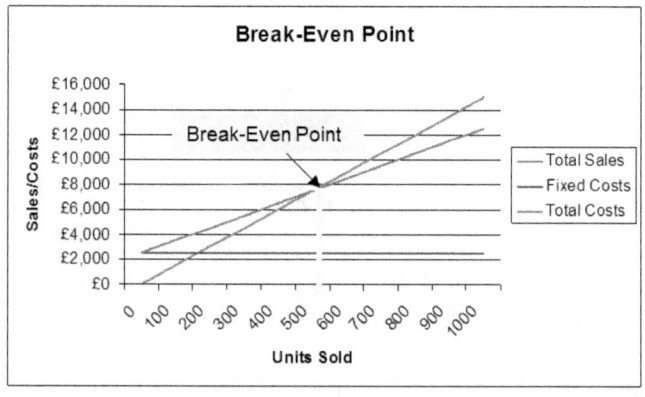

Projected Balance Sheet

The balance sheet provides a snap shot of the assets and liabilities of your business at a certain point in time. It shows your business's assets such as land, building, stock and cash. It also shows what is owed to the business such as money from debtors. Additionally, it shows the liabilities of your business, that is, who your business owes money to such as suppliers, the bank, investors, etc. When producing a projected balance sheet, you need to include the following:

Fixed Assets – These are assets that provide a long-term benefit, for at least a year, which the business intends to keep. Examples of fixed assets are machinery, motor vehicles, office equipment, and buildings.

Current Assets – Those which will be used up or sold in the next year and the cash balances kept in the business. Current assets include the following:

Stocks (also known as inventories) which include finished goods, raw materials and work-in-progress.
Debtors who owe the business money
Cash in the bank and in the cash box

Current Liabilities – These are what the business owes in the short term. These include:

Creditors – Suppliers who are owed money by the business in the short term.
Bank Overdraft – Amounts due to be paid back to the bank within the next 12 months

Working Capital – This is the amount of money made available for the day to day running of the business. You calculate Working Capital by subtracting Current Liabilities from Current Assets. A negative figure for working capital means that the business has outstanding debts that need to be paid for, but the business is unable to do so because it does not have any cash to spare.

Long-Term Liabilities – Money borrowed by the business for much longer than a year. A good example of a long-term liability is a bank loan.

Share Capital – This is the money invested in the business by the owners.

Profit and Loss Reserves – Profits due to the owners of the business. The money may not be in the form of cash, but was used to purchase more stock or fixed assets.

Capital – This is the amount of long-term money invested in the business by the owner to purchase assets. Besides the owner's money, capital could also be in the form of long-term bank loans.

Example of a Balance Sheet Projection:

	A	B
Assets		
Current Assets		
Cash in bank	5,000	
Accounts receivable	15,300	
Inventory	30,000	
Total Current Assets	50,300	
Fixed Assets		
Land and Building	150,000	
Motor Vehicle	7,000	
Furniture	1,850	
Total Fixed Assets	158,850	
TOTAL ASSETS	209,150	
Liabilities and Equity		
Current Liabilities		
Bank Overdraft	20,000	
Creditors	15,000	
Total Current Liabilities	35,000	
Long-Term Debt		
Bank loans payable	80,000	
Total Long-Term Debt	80,000	
TOTAL LIABILITIES	115,000	
Owner's Equity		
Invested Capital	94,150	
Total Owner's Equity	94,150	
TOTAL LIABILITIES & EQUITY	209,150	

Whether you are starting a new business or are trying to grow an existing one, it is imperative that you have a business plan. Don't just write a business plan because you want to apply for a bank loan or to attract investors. Your business plan should be a guide that shows you how you can optimize growth and development of your business according to your priorities. Follow the above guidelines to write a successful business plan for your online business.

Chapter 9: Accounting for Online Business

This is the part of your business that you may feel ill-equipped at doing, but it is mandatory by law that you keep financial records of any income you receive so that you can fill in your tax return and show that your figures are correct. Keeping good accounting records will help you to make wise financial decisions and run your business more efficiently.

Don't worry. You don't have to be a professional accountant to keep proper records. And you don't necessarily have to buy expensive software either. You can use free programs such as Microsoft Excel and software you can download from the internet to record your income and expenses such as:

http://www.turbocashuk.com
http://www.gnucash.org
http://www.mybrightbook.com

But it is always best to get training in the skill you will need to keep good financial records. Furthermore, you could always hire an accountant to keep records of your business for you when your business grows and you have a steady revenue coming in. But you should at least acquire some basic knowledge of accounting.

Accounting Records to Keep for Your Online Business

Because you are self-employed you are required to keep at least the following records:

Invoices for sales and purchases
Receipts for business expenses
Bank records

You also have to choose an accounting method that is suitable for your online business. An accounting method is a set of rules used to determine when and how income and expenses are reported. You choose an accounting method for your business when you file your first tax return. You can choose between the following two basic accounting methods:

Cash Method – you report income in the tax year you receive it. Normally you deduct or capitalize expenses in the tax year you pay them.

Accrual Method – you generally report income in the tax year you earn it, although you have not received any cash yet. Under the accrual method, you deduct or capitalize expenses in the tax year you incur them, whether or not you pay them that year.

You have to use the same accounting method to calculate your taxable income and to keep proper financial records. The accounting method you choose must clearly show your income and you cannot switch between accounting methods every tax year. You have to stick with the same method.

If you have already set up an accounting system and you realize that the accounting method you chose for your business is unsuitable, then you need to seek approval from HMRC if you live in the UK or from the IRS if you live outside of the UK.

How to Keep Financial Records

It is essential to every business to keep proper financial records of all the daily transactions of the business. Keeping good records of your business will help you to do the following:

Monitor the growth of your business. Keeping good records will show whether your business is improving, what items are selling, and what changes need to be made.

Prepare your financial statements. You need to keep proper records in order to prepare accurate financial statements such as income statements and balance sheets. These statements can help you to get a loan from the bank, to deal with creditors and to manage your business effectively.

Identify source of receipts. Your business will receive money or property from many different sources and your records will help you to identify the source of your receipts. You will need this information so that you can separate business from non-business receipts and taxable from non-taxable income.

Prepare your tax returns. You need to keep accurate records of your income, expenses, and credits so that you may be able to prepare your tax returns.

Support items reported on your tax returns. Keep a complete set of financial records available at all times so that you will be able to explain any items reported on your tax returns when HMRC or IRS inspects your records.

When you start keeping financial records of your business you will need evidence of your business transactions. This evidence comes in the form of supporting documents. Sales, purchases, payroll and other transactions that occur in your business usually generate supporting documents. These documents include sales slips, paid bills, invoices, receipts, deposit slips, and cancelled checks. These supporting documents contain all the information you need to record in your books and will support your tax return.

The income you receive from your business may come in the form of gross receipts. Your supporting documents usually show the amounts and sources of your gross receipts and these normally come in the form of cash register tapes, bank deposit slips, receipt books, invoices, and credit card charge slips.

Purchases are items you buy and resell to your customers. The purchases you make for your business are shown on the supporting documents which contain the amount paid and that the amount was for purchases. The supporting documents you need for business purchases are cancelled checks, cash register tape receipts, credit card sales slips, and invoices.

You also need to keep record of the expenses, other than purchases, you incur to continue operating your business. Your supporting documents should show what business expense the amount was for and how much was paid. Cancelled checks, cash register tapes, account statements, credit card sales slips, invoices, and petty cash slips for small cash payments are all examples of supporting documents you can use to record your business expenses.

One other financial record you need to keep for your business is a record of your assets. Property, machinery, office equipment, and furniture are all examples of assets that you own and use in your business. You need to keep accurate records of your assets in order to calculate the annual depreciation and the gain or loss when you sell your assets. Your financial records should show the following information:

1. When and how you acquired the asset
2. The purchase price of the asset
3. The cost of any improvements made to the asset
4. Deductions taken for depreciation
5. Deductions taken for losses resulting from fires or storms
6. How you used the asset
7. How and when you disposed of the asset
8. Selling price of the asset
9. Expenses incurred in the sale of the asset

The supporting documents that may show this information are purchase and sales invoices, real estate closing statements, and cancelled checks.

How to Record Business Transactions

When keeping financial records of your business it is essential that you include a summary of all your business transactions. Evidence of your business transactions are shown on supporting documents. You can record business transactions in special books called journals and ledgers. You can also record your business transactions in a spreadsheet program using Excel on your computer.

A journal is where you record each business transaction shown on your supporting documents. You can have separate journals for transactions which occur frequently. A ledger, however, contains the totals from all of your journals which are organized into different accounts.

How you keep your journals and ledgers depends on the type of business you are in. For example, a typical small business may keep a record keeping system which includes the following items:

1. Business check book
2. Daily summary of cash receipts
3. Monthly summary of cash receipts
4. Check disbursements (expenses) journal
5. Depreciation worksheet
6. Employee compensation record

For the purpose of your online business, I will show you a basic method of keeping records of all your business transactions.

When you start your business the first thing you should do is open a business checking account to keep your business transactions separate from your personal transactions.

Your business check book is your basic source of information for keeping track of your business expenses. It is highly recommended that you deposit all daily receipts to your business account as soon as possible. You should always make payments by check to document your business expenses.

The only time you should write a check to yourself is when you are withdrawing money from your business account for personal use. Make sure that you use your business account for business purposes only.

The following are examples of how you can keep accurate financial records of your online business.

For your online business, the main records you should keep are:

1. Sales Journal
2. Expenses Journal
3. Profit and Loss (Income) Statement
4. Cash Flow Statement

Example of a Sales Journal:

Date	TOTAL SALES	E-Book	Advertising	Paid Subscriptions	E-Course
01/05/2012	1,500	200	500	500	300
02/05/2012	2,000	500	1,000	200	300
03/05/2012	5,000	500	2,000	2,000	500
04/05/2012	6,000	1,000	3,000	3,000	1,000
05/05/2012	7,000	1,000	1,000	1,000	2,000
06/05/2012	6,000	1,500	1,500	1,500	1,500
07/05/2012	4,500	500	1,000	1,500	1,000
08/05/2012	1,000	200	200	200	200
09/05/2012	2,500	200	300	1,000	1,000
10/05/2012	3,000	500	1,000	1,000	500
TOTAL	38,500	6,100	11,500	11,900	8,300

Example of an Expenses Journal:

Date	Paid To	Check #	EXPENSES	Web Hosting	Rent	Utilities	Telephone	Internet	Office Supplies	Travel
01/05/2012	Landlord	543	500		500					
02/05/2012	Mobile Phone		10				10			
03/05/2012	Internet	547	21					21		
04/05/2012	Web Host		100	100						
05/05/2012	Utilities	550	1,000			1,000				
06/05/2012	Stationary	551	150						150	
07/05/2012	Mobile Phone		25				25			
08/05/2012	Petrol		50							50
09/05/2012	Stationary	556	250						250	
10/05/2012	Petrol		20							20
TOTAL			2,126	100	500	1,000	35	21	400	70

Example of Profit and Loss (Income) Statement:

Sales	£
e-Book	6,100
Advertising	11,500
Paid Subscriptions	11,900
e-Course	8,300
Total Sales	**37,800**
Expenses	
Web Hosting	100
Rent	500
Utilities	1000
Telephone	35
Internet	21
Office Supplies	400
Travel	70
Total Expenses	**2,126**
Net Profit	**35,674**

Example of a Cash Flow Statement:

Beginning Balance	£27,000
Cash In (this month)	£35,200
Cash Out (this month)	£-1,126
Ending Cash Balance	£61,074

So you can see from the examples above that it is very easy to keep financial records of your business.

Chapter 10: How to Make Money From Your Site

If you have been following the steps detailed in this book then by now you should have come up with a brilliant business idea, written your business plan, registered a domain name, built your website or blog, promoted your online business, and started keeping records of your business's income and expenses (not necessarily in that order). If you haven't achieved all of these steps yet then don't worry. You can work at your own pace in your own time.

Now we come to this section that you may find very interesting, that is, how to make money from your website or blog and how to keep the cash rolling in long after you have put in all the time and effort to create your internet business. You need to understand how to monetize your site so that you can generate monthly streams of revenue long after you have created and marketed your website.

How would you like to receive continuous income for a job that you only had to do once? Imagine receiving recurring income long after you have stopped working. This type of income is known as passive residual income.

Passive Residual Income

If you would like to retire early, take your family on a luxury cruise, or stay home to take care of the kids, then in order for all this to happen, you need to create a passive residual income. This type of income can be achieved by investing your time and money into your online business and by implementing some or all of the following income streams:

Join affiliate programs. I had mentioned this in previous chapters, but this is a great way to make money without having to go through all the effort of creating a product of your own. And this is one of the ways that you can build passive residual income. If you already have your website set up then you can earn passive income by pre-selling another company's products. Anytime a customer purchases a product through your website, the merchant tracks the sale and pays you a commission for each sale.

Search for companies that offer large commissions and that track sales for a long period of time, that is, for a lifetime. Just to get you started, here is a list of affiliate directories and programs you can join for free:

Clickbank http://www.clickbank.com
Affiliate Window http://www.affiliatewindow.com
Commission Junction http://www.cj.com
Linkshare http://www.linkshare.com

Create information products to sell. While you are generating revenue from your affiliate products, you can spend time creating your own information products to sell from your website or blog. An e-book, for example, is a great information product that is easy to produce.

You can create an e-book that teaches people how to do stuff, for example, how to create a website, how to get out of debt, or how to start a home based business. People are hungry for information and they are looking for solutions that make life easier for them.

An e-book is easy to create and is low cost. When people buy your e-book from your site, you get to keep 100% of the profits. You can also add an affiliate program so that other people can sell your e-book for a commission. You can do this easily by joining Clickbank as a Vendor. By increasing the number of e-book sales through your affiliates you also increase your passive income.

Sell advertising space on your website. If you have hundreds or even thousands of visitors to your site each day then you can offer other companies to place a banner ad or a text link on your site for a monthly fee.

Selling advertising space on your website is made easy by using the Komoona plugin that you can install on your Wordpress website. Go to http://www.komoona.com to get started. You only have to set it up once and then collect the passive residual income. You can also place banner ads and text links in your newsletter that people subscribe to and in your e-books.

Make money with Google Adsense. You can also sign up for Google Adsense and place Google ads on your site which pays you a commission every time someone clicks on the ad. Visit the following link to find out how to create a Google Adsense account:

http://support.google.com/affiliatenetwork/publisher/answer/156883?hl=en

To actually join Google's Affiliate Network then you
need to click on the following link:

http://www.google.co.uk/ads/affiliatenetwork

**Charge a monthly membership fee to gain access to
your site.** Over time, because of all the research you have
done online and because of all the books you have read,
you may become an expert in your field. With this
knowledge, you can create a membership site in which
you charge subscribers a monthly fee to gain access to all
of the resources, products, and support you offer on your
site. The more members that subscribe to your site, the
more money you make. The added advantage to being an
expert in your field is that you can also recommend
affiliate products to your members from which you earn
commissions.

Resell other people's services. A good example of this is
domain registration or web hosting. You pay a monthly
fee to the company and then you can set your own price
for the service you intend to offer your customers.
Bluehost.com and Hostgator.com are two good examples
of how you can resell web hosting services. However,
you need to ensure that you are thoroughly
knowledgeable about the service you offer so that you
can provide support to your customers. By reselling other
people's services, you can earn ongoing residual income.

Monetizing your website to create passive residual
income streams is a great way to secure your financial
future. These days you can never be too sure about the
future. You never know if you will be made redundant

from your job, feel too sick to work, experience a disaster in your life, or if you want to start saving for retirement.

It is never too soon to start preparing for your financial future. So get started now by choosing any of the above passive income streams to secure your financial future.

Internet Business Action Plan

We have covered a lot of topics in starting your own online business that it may be a little overwhelming. There is so much to do that you may be wondering what you should do first. For this reason, I put together a quick start 10 step action plan to help you get started, step by step, to set up your internet business.

Step 1
Come up with a profitable idea. You can get ideas from your hobbies, work experience, specialized knowledge or from other people's problems.

Step 2
Identify your target market. Describe the type of customer you want to sell to.

Step 3
Carry out your market research. Find out what products, services or information are in demand using Google's Keyword Tool. Use Google Search, Clickbank, Amazon and eBay to analyze the competition and to determine the profitability of your chosen market.

Step 4
Decide what you are going to sell. You can either sell your own product or other people's products through affiliate marketing, or do both. Sign up for affiliate programs by joining Amazon's Associates, Clickbank, or eBay's affiliate program.

Step 5

Create a website or blog. Register your domain name at Domainorb.com, set up web hosting at Justhost.com, and design your website or blog using Wordpress. You also have the option of setting up an email autoresponder for your site.

Step 6

Create an e-commerce website. You can either install a Wordpress e-commerce plugin or join Amazon Associates to set up Amazon's aStore on your website.

Step 7

Promote your website by using the following marketing methods:

1. Optimize your site with relevant keywords using Google's Keyword Tool.
2. Submit your site to search engines like Google, Bing and Yahoo!
3. Submit your content to article directories such as Ezinearticles.com and Goarticles.com.
4. Place an ad on free classified ads sites.
5. Create and email a newsletter to visitors who subscribe to your site.
6. Create a video and submit it to Youtube.com and other video sites.
7. Write a press release and submit it to press release sites like Prweb.com.
8. Join online forums and include a link to your website in your resource box.

9. Create a slideshow and submit it to Slideshare.com and Scribd.com.
10. Promote your affiliate links or your website with PLR content and submit it to e-book directories.
11. Market your site on social networks like Linkedin.com and Facebook.com.
12. Create a Facebook fan page to promote your own products as well as affiliate products.
13. Market your site offline with business cards and advertising in newspapers.

Step 8
Register your business and write a business plan.

Step 9
Set up accounting records to keep track of the income generated and expenses incurred for your online business.

Step 10
Generate lifetime riches by monetizing your website or blog to produce continuous income for a lifetime.

Conclusion

I have read so many books and did a lot of research on building an online business, internet marketing, and affiliate programs, but I waited a whole year before I finally made a commitment to starting my own online business. Now that I have my own website and have created my own products to sell online, I wish that I had started earlier. I wish that I did not wait a whole year to start my online business.

But my story does not have to be yours. You bought this book so it means that you are interested in starting and running a successful online business. It means that you are ready to start generating multiple streams of income from your website. Even before you finish reading this book, you can begin the process of creating your products, building your website, and marketing your internet business.

I hope that this guide has helped you to see the possibility of making huge profits by starting an online business. The sooner you start, the greater the rewards will be. So take action now. Follow the steps in this book and you will soon be on your way to generating a steady income stream on the internet.

About the Author

Christine John holds a BSc degree in Management Studies and is an experienced writer, web designer and entrepreneur. Today she lives in the United Kingdom where she helps authors, aspiring entrepreneurs, and individuals to create and grow their business on the internet.

Questions for the Author?
Email me at christinejohnbooks@gmail.com

One Last Thing…
Thank you for taking the time to read my book. I do hope that you learned a lot about starting and running an online business. If you have friends or family members who you believe would benefit from reading this book then I would be grateful if you could post your thoughts on Facebook or Twitter. I would also be honoured if you posted a review of my book on Amazon.